THE SECOND
BARONS' WAR

THE SECOND BARONS' WAR

SIMON DE MONTFORT AND THE BATTLES OF LEWES AND EVESHAM

JOHN SADLER

You only have to play at Little Wars a few times
to realise what a blundering thing Great Wars must be.
H.G. Wells

Pen & Sword
MILITARY

First published in Great Britain in 2008 by
Pen & Sword Military
An imprint of
Pen & Sword Books Ltd
47 Church Street
Barnsley
South Yorkshire
S70 2AS

Copyright © John Sadler, 2008

ISBN 978 1 84415 831 7

A CIP catalogue record for this book is
available from the British Library.

Typeset in 11.5pt Ehrhardt

Printed and bound in England
by Biddles

Pen & Sword Books Ltd incorporates the imprints of
Pen & Sword Aviation, Pen & Sword Maritime, Pen & Sword Military,
Wharncliffe Local History, Pen & Sword Select,
Pen & Sword Military Classics and Leo Cooper.

For a complete list of Pen & Sword titles please contact
PEN & SWORD BOOKS LIMITED
47 Church Street, Barnsley, South Yorkshire, S70 2AS, England
E-mail: enquiries@pen-and-sword.co.uk
Website: www.pen-and-sword.co.uk

Contents

Preface and Acknowledgements

The 'death of chivalry', a description applied to the Battle of Evesham, is an emotive title, especially to any of my generation who was brought up on fifties and early sixties children's TV programmes such as *Knights of the Round Table*, *Robin Hood* (the version with Richard Greene in the title role), *William Tell* and, of course, *Ivanhoe* – Roger Moore in his pre 'Saint' days. These went in tandem with reading such books as the Puffin version of *Knights of the Round Table* by Roger Lancelyn-Green, the novels of Rosemary Sutcliff, Henry Treece and survivors from G.A. Henty, Stevenson and Dumas, naturally. Knighthood and the manly virtues of chivalry were paramount, and the medieval tradition was carried forward by Biggles, Beau Geste and Karl the Viking.

Nowadays I imagine all of these are frowned upon as extolling the unfashionable or, worse, 'inappropriate' ideals of elitism, militarism and imperialism and, along with Enid Blyton, have been banished by the dead hand of political correctness. Now, even the most ardent romantic amongst us must concede that the Middle Ages and medieval warfare were neither pretty nor honourable; the battles of which I will write hereafter were savage and bloody, merciless, cruel and vicious. Virtue and compassion are hard to detect.

Sword and lance will, nonetheless, continue to smack far more of honour than a cruise missile or thermobaric bomb. Medieval battles were at least fought over small areas, generally without any long-term, detrimental impact – the odd pile of bones to be sure, but these are bio-degradable. Most of those who fought were household men or mercenaries; armies were far fewer in number and the bulk of casualties by far were the combatants themselves. This is not to say that war was gentlemanly; it was not. It was, however, more gentlemanly and less destructive than today. The profession of arms was the only career route open to a gentleman of birth, bar the church, and quite frequently leading prelates managed to combine the mace and the mitre quite seamlessly, Anthony Bek, the Prince Bishop of Durham in Edward I's reign, being a significant example.

The events described here of the early and mid-thirteenth century were pivotal to the social and cultural history of Britain. Magna Carta, the core concept of consensual government, as opposed to the unfettered exercise of the royal prerogative, was a key step in the country's political history, shaping the way the British live today. Whether those fathers of what became democratic rule would recognize the government of today is hard to assess. It is inconceivable they could applaud a generation of politicians so irretrievably enmired in 'spin' and venality, though corruption and nepotism were scarcely unknown in their day.

A note on money: in the thirteenth century the pound sterling comprised twenty shillings, each of twelve pennies, but marks were also used, being equal to two-thirds of the value of the pound, i.e. thirteen shillings and four pence. Attempts to provide comparative values are particularly fraught and must be treated with caution. At this time a wealthy magnate of the first rank might enjoy an annual income of, say, £5,000 per annum; knights were paid at the rate of £2 per diem and the lowly foot a mere two pence.

During the early thirteenth century a pernicious practice had arisen of 'clipping' or counterfeiting coins; overseas money-changers who, like jackals, followed papal tax-collectors and itinerant merchants were not well regarded. This continual debasement of the English coinage aroused much ire. Henry III certainly attempted to curtail these practices and declared that every penny must be of standard weight and size. Jewish money-lenders were much blamed, justly or otherwise. Coin was the currency, primarily, of the urban commercial bourgeoisie; the knights of the shires probably saw relatively little. Paper money of course and promissory notes were unknown.

In writing this present volume I am indebted to the following for their generous assistance: Rupert Harding and Philip Sidnell at Pen & Sword; Chloe Rodham, who drew the maps; the staff of the National Archives, Royal Armouries, Leeds; the Wallace Collection; and the Almonry at Evesham. Rosie Serdiville and Philip Walling for proofreading and trenchant editorial advice; Ed Wimble; Catherine Turner of Durham Cathedral Library; Iain Dickie and Michael Rayner of the Battlefields Trust; Tony Whiting of Evesham Tourist Centre; John Wollaston; Beryl Charlton; and particularly Tony Spicer, who has been most generous with his researches. Lastly, and as ever, I am indebted to my wife for her continuing patience during the gestation and birth of yet another history.

Any errors or omissions are, of course, and remain my sole responsibility.

John Sadler
Northumberland, winter 2007–2008

Dedication

This one is for Philip

List of Illustrations

The Almonry. This monastic survivor now houses an information centre and battle room.

St Lawrence's Church. The Abbey Park marks the muster point for the Montfortians on the morning of the battle.

The Abbey Tower. This survives (altered since the thirteenth century) in the Abbey Park in the centre of the modern town.

Green Hill, looking eastwards toward the field. Edward's division would have been deployed on the left and de Clare's on the right.

Green Hill, looking westwards back towards the town. It was up the line of the present High Street that de Montfort's knights rode on the day of the battle.

The Leicester Tower. Built by Edward Rudge in 1842, it is said to be based on Guy's Tower at Warwick Castle.

The Leicester Tower commemorative plaque.

The Obelisk, north panel.

The Obelisk, east panel. 'I am Henry of Winchester your King: Do not kill me.'

The Obelisk, south panel.

The Obelisk, west panel.

The Obelisk viewed from the north. Rudge also erected the pleasingly proportioned Obelisk, now obscured by planting.

The field, viewed from the Squires. This is looking south and east from the Squires.

View of the Downs above Lewes. A general view showing the rolling terrain.

View of the Downs. A further view showing the high ground above the town.

Modern Lewes. A view of the townscape.

The barbican. The castle barbican viewed from the main street.

View through the barbican taken looking though the gateway, giving an impression of the narrowness of the town's medieval thoroughfares.

View of the castle. The motte and bailey form of construction is plainly visible.

View of the field from the castle. The green space to the left is the Paddock where Edward's cavalry mustered.

View from the castle walls looking up toward the Downs.

Two views of the ruins of St Pancras' Priory.

Maps

Timeline

1215   Signing of Magna Carta; outbreak of First Barons' War

1216   First siege of Dover; sieges of Windsor and Rochester
October: death of King John

1217   Second siege of Dover; battles of Lincoln, Dover and
Sandwich
September: Treaty of Lambeth

1230?   Simon de Montfort arrives in England

1238   Simon marries Eleanor of England

1242   Battle of Taillebourg

1258   Provisions of Oxford

1261   Henry III obtains a papal bull releasing him from the
Provisions of Oxford

1263   Simon de Montfort identified as leader of baronial faction

1264   January: Louis IX delivers arbitration verdict in King
Henry's favour
Spring: hostilities begin
3 April: the king raises his standard at Oxford
5 April: Northampton falls to the king
11 April: the royal army at Leicester
17 April: Rochester besieged by Montfortians
19 April: city of Rochester taken, but the castle-keep
holds out
The king celebrates Easter Day (20 April) at Nottingham
26 April: the king reaches Croydon
28/29 April: the king at Rochester
4?/8 May: the king at Winchelsea
9 May: the king at Battle; Montfortians on the march from
London
11 May: the royal army at Lewes; baronial forces at
Fletching, eight miles to the north
14 May: Battle of Lewes, King Henry and Prince Edward
captive; de Montfort in control

15 May: the Mise of Lewes concluded

June: constitution established by de Montfort in place; the council of nine

1265   January: first meeting of the English Parliament in the Palace of Westminster

April: de Montfort at odds with de Clare; splits in the baronial faction

8 May: de Montfort at Hereford with the king and Prince Edward

28 May: Prince Edward escapes from captivity

19 June: de Montfort concludes negotiations with Llywelwyn of Wales

14? June: royalists take Gloucester (castle holds out till 29 June); Simon the Younger still before Pevensey

24 June: de Montfort moves to Monmouth

2 July: Montfortians reach Usk

4 July: baronial forces attain Newport

10 July: de Montfort, his ships taken or destroyed, abandons Newport

11 July: Montfortians at Hay-on-Wye

16 July: the baronial army returns to Hereford; the younger Simon sacks Winchester

31 July: Simon the Younger arrives at Kenilworth

1 August: Edward becomes aware of the baronial army around Kenilworth

2 August: Edward carries out spoiling raid, beating up the baronial army's quarters and capturing key magnates

3 August: Edward marches back to Worcester; Simon senior is at Kempsey, marches for Evesham at dusk

4 August: Simon senior reaches Evesham around 5 am. The royalists begin to come up thereafter and the battle starts around 9 am.

4 August: the Battle of Evesham – the death of chivalry

1266   October: terms agreed with the surviving rebels; the dictum of Kenilworth

1267   End of the war, terms of the dictum of Kenilworth ratified

1272   Death of Henry III; accession of Edward I.

Dramatis Personae

Adam Marsh (c.1200–1259)
An English Franciscan, leading academic and theologian; studied under Robert Grosseteste (see below); spiritual counsellor to Simon de Montfort, sixth Earl of Leicester; also an accomplished jurist, consulted by both court and reformers as a leading lawyer and theologian.

Amaury VI de Montfort (1195–1241)
Son of Simon de Montfort, fifth Earl of Leicester; older brother of Simon de Montfort; fought in the Albigensian Crusade and inherited (for a period) the County of Toulouse; became Constable of France; also fought in the Sixth Crusade, was captured and died shortly after his release.

Amaury de Montfort, Canon of York (1242/1243–1301)
Fourth son of the sixth Earl of Leicester; spent his career in the priesthood and held a number of important offices, including that of papal chaplain.

Aymer de Valence, Bishop of Winchester (c.1222–1260)
A member of the Lusignan dynasty, half-brother to Henry III. Aymer and his brothers William de Valence and Geoffrey and Guy de Lusignan, jointly labelled the Lusignans, were distinguished by their perceived rapacity and propensity for violence. Aymer's mother was Isabella of Angouleme, King John's second wife. He and his brothers came to England in 1247 seeking advancement. He first obtained a prebend in the diocese of London before being raised to his bishopric; repudiated the Provisions of Oxford; was besieged and obliged to accept exile; died in Paris.

Edmund Crouchback, first Earl of Lancaster (1245–1296)
The second son of Henry III and Eleanor of Provence; younger

brother of Edward; became Earl of Leicester after the title was attainted; besieged Kenilworth after Evesham. It was for him that Henry III expended much effort and treasure to secure the crown of Sicily.

Edward I of England, 'Longshanks' (1239–1307)
In his mid-twenties was de Montfort's natural opponent, though he seems to have maintained respect for the earl. Longshanks clearly learnt from his rashness at Lewes, and his conduct of the Evesham campaign, unfettered by his father, the king, was masterly and brought the baronial army to the field in greatly advantageous circumstances.

Eleanor of England (1215–1275)
Wife of Simon de Montfort; youngest child of John and Isabella of Angouleme. Married at a very young age to William Marshal, she subsequently swore an oath of chastity which was to seriously exercise Simon in the course of their marriage, though she bore him seven surviving children. After the death of her husband and eldest son at Evesham, she fled to France and subsequently entered a nunnery.

Eleanor of Provence (1223–1291)
Queen consort to Henry III, to whom she was married in 1236; daughter of the Count of Provence; bore the king five surviving children (though the youngest daughter, Katherine, died aged only four); her Savoyard relations were unpopular and she was herself attacked by the London mob in 1263. She was particularly devoted to Edward, her eldest son, and the prince conceived a deep resentment against the Londoners for the slight – he took a fearful toll of them at Lewes in consequence.

Gilbert de Clare, seventh Earl of Hertford, third Earl of Gloucester (1243–1295)
A noted reformer and, like de Montfort, virulently anti-Semitic; he led the massacre of Jews at Canterbury in April 1264, prior to Lewes, where he fought on the side of the barons.

Excommunicated in October; he and de Montfort quarrelled and the split was a major factor in the renewal of hostilities in 1265. His first wife was Alice de Lusignan, sister to the Lusignan brothers, so unpopular in the reforming period 1258–1263.

Guy de Montfort, Count of Nola (1244–1288)
Son of Simon de Montfort, sixth earl. Wounded at Evesham, the battle wherein both his father and elder brother Henry died, he was held till the following spring at Windsor, from where, having bribed his gaolers, he was able to escape to France. He served under Charles of Anjou and fought well in the Battle of Alba, excommunicated after his murder of Henry of Almain, a crime committed with his brother Simon de Montfort the Younger. Guy was captured in 1287 by the Aragonese after the Battle of the Counts, and died in captivity the following year.

Henry of Almain (1235–1271)
Son of Richard of Cornwall and Isabel Marshal; nephew of both Henry III and Simon de Montfort; captured after fighting on the royalist side at Lewes. He took the cross with Prince Edward in 1268 but was sent back to deal with fresh disturbances in Gascony; murdered at prayer in Viterbo on 13 March 1271 by Guy and Simon de Montfort the Younger, a crime which shocked European nobility and led to excoriation of the de Montforts.

Henry III of England (1207–1272)
Son of John 'Lackland'; perceived as extravagant and impulsive; censored for advancing foreign favourites, his wife's Savoyard kin and his own Lusignan half-brothers. His alleged misrule finally provoked action by the 'Reformers' in 1258. This and the subsequent Provisions of Oxford led directly to the outbreak of civil war.

Henry de Montfort (1238–1265)
Eldest of Simon de Montfort's brood of sons; 'your presumption and the pride of your brothers has brought me to this end', his father is said to have rebuked him on the morning of their last

battle at Evesham. Like his parent, he perished in the fight. He was named to please the king – Henry was not a familial name; Simon, Guy or Amaury were more common.

Hugh le Despenser (Despencer), first Baron le Despencer (1223–1265)

Husband of Aline Bassett, daughter of Philip Bassett, another leading reformer. Served as Justiciar of England in 1260 and also held the important office of Constable of the Tower of London. He fell at Evesham, allegedly by the hand of Roger Mortimer, a deed which engendered a smouldering feud between the two families.

Humphrey de Bohun, second Earl of Hereford (1208–1275)

One of Prince Edward's godfathers; also, after returning from crusade, one of the authors of the Provisions of Oxford; married to Maud de Lusignan, he remained a royalist. His son Humphrey de Bohun fought on the baronial side and led the doomed advance of the foot at Evesham; both had previously been on the field of Lewes on opposing sides.

Llywelwyn ap Gruffydd, or Llywelwyn the Last (1223–1282)

The last free prince of the Welsh before the Edwardian conquest and his own subsequent death in combat. He had previously sworn fealty to Henry III. Much of his energies in the 1250s were devoted to internecine squabbles. He lent support to de Montfort and offered 30,000 marks in consideration for a permanent Anglo-Welsh truce and recognition of his titles. A formal alliance was agreed by the terms of Pipton in June 1265; he sent a body of Welsh spears to support the baronial cause.

Peter de Montfort (c.1215–1265)

A staunch supporter of de Montfort who joined him in death at Evesham. There was a family connection through joint ancestry and Peter is credited as being the first presiding officer or 'prolocutor' of the Commons, now the office of the Speaker.

Richard, first Earl of Cornwall (1209–1272)

Younger brother of Henry III; Count of Poitou and, from 1257, 'King of the Romans'; in 1231 married Isabel Marshal, widow of the Earl of Gloucester, to his brother's disapproval. He had quarrelled with de Montfort over the latter's marriage to Eleanor in 1238 and the feud simmered. His second wife was the queen's sister Sanchia of Provence. He had the good sense to avoid the fatal lure of Sicily and showed little interest in his German title, even after bribing the electors. After his capture at Lewes he was imprisoned and played little part in the remainder of the fighting.

Robert de Ferrers, sixth Earl of Derby (1239–1279)

At an early age married to one of the daughters of Hugh XI of Lusignan, Count de la Marche, eldest of Henry III's half-brothers. As Robert was a minor when his father died, he was made a royal ward; Prince Edward sold this wardship on to Peter of Savoy, possibly the cause of the antipathy which arose between him and Edward. The sixth earl had a vast estate but his espousal of the baronial faction, largely dictated by self-interest, was to cost him dear; the bulk of his confiscated lands passed to what would become the Duchy of Lancaster. He died without recovering more than a small portion of his original inheritance.

Robert Grosseteste (c.1175–1253)

A leading theologian, acknowledged diplomat and churchman; Bishop of Lincoln; a towering intellect with a strong interest in scientific matters; particular friend to Adam Marsh and advisor to de Montfort. It was he who, in 1239, sought to heal the breach with Henry III. A noted advocate of church reform, he was not a secularist but still opposed Henry's policy of alignment with the papacy.

Roger Mortimer, first Baron Wigmore (1231–1282)

One of the great marcher lords, sometimes ally to and sometimes enemy of the Welshman Llywelyn (his mother, Gwladys, was the daughter of Llywelyn the Great); remained consistently loyal to Henry III. His wife Maud was also of joint Anglo-Welsh stock, and it was Mortimer who was credited with killing both Simon de Montfort and Hugh Despenser at Evesham.

Simon de Montfort, fifth Earl of Leicester (1160–1218)

Member of a dynasty hailing from Montfort l'Amaury near Paris; married Alix de Montmorency; his mother was Amicia de Beaumont, daughter of the third Earl of Leicester. King John assumed possession of de Montfort's Beaumont inheritance, and Simon sought fame in the Albigensian Crusade after 1209. His extreme piety and harshness, combined with a considerable talent for generalship, won success and renown; he became one of the leading captains of his day, and was killed at the siege of Toulouse.

Simon de Montfort, sixth Earl of Leicester (1208–1265)

Leader of the reformers from 1258 and mainstay of the baronial faction until his death in battle at Evesham; distinguished by his extreme religiosity and perceived integrity. Always respected as a soldier, he was also always prone to excessive avarice and pronounced self-interest. Blunt and disputatious, he lacked the finesse necessary to wield political power effectively and alienated a number of key supporters, most particularly Gilbert de Clare, Earl of Gloucester.

Simon de Montfort (the Younger) (1240–1271)

The second son of the sixth earl, who appears to have blamed the rapacity of his sons for the ruin of his cause. Simon the Younger commanded the debacle at Kenilworth but missed Evesham. He and his brother Guy murdered Henry of Almain in 1271; outcast and reviled, Simon died in obscurity the same year.

Walter de Cantilupe, Bishop of Worcester (d. 1266)

An itinerant justiciar in the early years of Henry III, from a family traditionally loyal to the crown; elected to the see of Worcester in 1236 and quickly became identified with the ecclesiastical reformers. After Grosseteste's death he became the leading voice of the movement and emerged as an ally of the Montfortians. Though a lesser intellect than his mentor, he was widely and well regarded by all sides as being a man of integrity. After Evesham he lapsed into genteel obscurity and died the following year.

William de Valence, first Earl of Pembroke (1225–1296)

Born Guillaume de Lusignan, fourth son of John's widow Queen Isabella of Angouleme by her subsequent marriage to Hugh X of Lusignan, Count of La Marche. After the French took Poitou in 1246, William, with his brothers Aymer de Valence and Guy de Lusignan, came to England to the court of their half-brother Henry III. They enjoyed great favour and advancement to the rising resentment of the English magnates who found they did not much care for these upstart Lusignans, notably arrogant and imbued with a propensity for the use of force. William soon quarrelled with de Montfort. Having refused to accept the Provisions of Oxford he was hounded out, though he returned to fight for the king at Lewes before being forced, once again, to flee to France.

Chapter 1

Background: Of Arms and Men

We have made a covenant with death,
and with hell are we at agreement.
Isaiah xxviii. 15

War was the profession of a gentleman; that urge which may motivate young men or women to enter Sandhurst now is an echo of chivalry and the roots of a knightly code which may be detected in Homer, as the Trojan Sarpedon explains to his friend Glaucos:

> Why have you and I the seat of honour at home Glaucos? Why do we have the best portions, cups always full, and all treat us like something greater than men? And that fine estate on the banks of Xanthos, orchards and wheatlands of the best? For that we are bound to stand now before our people in the scorching fires of battle.[1]

Simon de Montfort the elder, on perceiving Prince Edward's royalists deploying before the Battle of Evesham, is famously said to have remarked: 'By the arm of St. James, they have not learned that for themselves, but were taught it by me! May God have mercy on our souls, for our bodies are theirs.'[2] If so, then the pupil had significantly outstripped the master. The roots of chivalry lay in a mist-shrouded Teutonic past, sanctioned and effectively annexed by the church, the ritual of knighthood providing a core philosophy and set of values which, whilst by no means always adhered to, enhanced the mystique. Combined with long years of training and expensive equipment, this permitted the mounted knight to maintain his elite and largely unchallenged status as arbiter upon the battlefield.

Strategy and tactics

In 1181 Henry II, Prince Edward's great-grandfather and founder of the Angevin Empire, had sought to regulate military affairs in England by statute. His Assize of Arms specified the arms and armour to be borne by each degree, from gentleman to commons. Henry III, a king singularly unschooled in war, revisited this earlier legislation in 1242; Prince Edward, as king some four decades later, overhauled the regulations once again. Henry III, who was struggling to recruit sufficient knights, ordained that those whose incomes exceeded £20 should be liable for knight service; any who earned £15 were obliged to provide their own mounts, and £2 freeholders their own bows.[3] Knight service could be commuted upon payment of a fine or *scutage*, and there was at this stage no attempt to standardize kit. The militia were also reorganized in that commissions of array were introduced for the first time. County sheriffs, as commissioners, were authorized and charged with reviewing the able-bodied men of each county and selecting a certain number, suitably equipped according to their means, from each settlement, their rations provided or funded from the communal purse. This form of conscription was never popular and much abused – a tendency parodied by Shakespeare's Falstaff in Henry IV Part 1 – 'If I be not ashamed of my soldiers I am a soused gurnet. I have misused the King's press damnably.'

Military service was bound into the mesh of feudalism, into the complex raft of obligations which existed between king and magnate as tenant-in-chief, between lord and vassal. The feudal system has been likened to a pyramid, with the king at its apex and the various orders graded below, from tenants-in-chief, knights, through to the labouring and unfree classes whose obligation was toil rather than their swords. Military commitment arose from the act of homage offered by the vassal to his lord:[4] normally this was for 40 days per annum and the inferior served unwaged; for the magnate his corresponding duty to the monarch was expressed as *servitium debitum*.[5] After the expiry of the contracted period the vassal was entitled to expect wages; magnates might, however, continue to serve without remuneration, preferring to expect rewards when the campaign was successfully concluded.

The king was reliant upon the Wardrobe as the administrative engine to drive and victual his war effort: here senior civil servants, cofferers and controllers, kept accurate records of expenditure – the accountancy of war. They, or their representatives, frequently accompanied the army, bringing their own gaggle of servants, acolytes and baggage. Supply was all-important, as all armies march better on a full belly, and the effects of a dearth of provisions married to a dangerous excess of ale could be dire – brawling broke out between the English and Welsh contingents of Edward's army engaged in the Falkirk campaign.[6] Similar and sanguinary disturbances are recorded by the Hainaulter Jean le Bel,[7] who served in Edward III's abortive Weardale campaign, nearly 30 years later. Foodstuffs comprised staples such as bread and a mix of beans, peas and oatmeal – 'potage'. An army of several thousand men would require several hundred tons of supplies per week, fodder for horses and small beer to drink.

In the mid-thirteenth century the bulk of fighting in the field was undertaken by mailed and mounted knights. In the Evesham campaign of 1265 Prince Edward faced two baronial armies: that of the older Simon, which lay west of the Severn, and that of his son, which was before Pevensey. Edward moved at speed, pinning his westerly opponents back behind the formidable river barrier and burning the bridges. Gloucester was secured, and a rebel fleet at anchor in Bristol dealt with. De Montfort the Younger was hurrying westwards to his father's relief, advancing as far as Kenilworth. The prince, then at Worcester, well placed to strike a blow at either of his foes, beat up the rebel quarters at Kenilworth in a classic dawn raid, before turning back for the decisive encounter at Evesham. It is suggested that commanders of this era were lacking in strategic flair, but Edward's campaign would indicate otherwise. His dynamism is to be contrasted with his father's lacklustre performance in the earlier campaign leading to defeat at Lewes. As Sir Charles Oman, something of an admirer of Longshanks, observes, the essence of the campaign was the royalists' success in keeping the barrier of the Severn and in frustrating the baronial army under de Montfort's attempts to cross. The prince, having kept his enemies apart, then moved decisively against first one and then the other.

In considering tactics we should reflect on the outcome of the Battle of Muret, fought on 12 September 1213, when a small mounted force of mailed knights and sergeants under the elder Simon de Montfort's redoubtable father encountered a far larger confederate force of mixed horse and foot before the walls of the town. The fight was an episode in the vicious suppression of the Cathar heresy. De Montfort, leading an army mainly comprising the chivalry of northern France, had humbled the Count of Toulouse, and the counts of Foix and Comminges. It appeared by the end of the summer season in that year that the business was effectively at an end and Simon had disbanded most of his forces. King Peter II of Aragon, who viewed the Frenchman's conquests in Languedoc with some alarum, had mustered a force to relieve Raymond of Toulouse and his affinity. This intervention caught Simon somewhat off guard, and the Aragonese achieved some initial successes against his outposts, finally settling down before the immensely strong walls of Muret.

De Montfort could not allow this vital bastion to fall but, on summoning his available forces, he could muster barely a thousand horse. Undeterred, he marched to the town and threw his forces within the walls. It now appeared to the besiegers, vastly superior in numbers, particularly of infantry, that the affair would simply become bogged down in a protracted siege. Simon had other ideas: his contempt for his foes in general and Peter II in particular was considerable, and he perceived they might be vulnerable to a bold offensive. Accordingly he caused one of the main gates to be opened, as though heralding a sally, which, as anticipated, stimulated a swift response, with the attackers swarming in. Despite Raymond's suggestion, the besiegers had not fortified their camp; the Spanish knights ridiculed such caution – most injudicious hubris.

Deploying his mailed horsemen in three divisions, attacking not in sequence but in echelon, Simon swept upon the flank of his adversaries, his first line breaking the confederates hastily thrown against them. The king and his knights now joined the fight against the first two lines but Simon and the third descended like the wrath of God upon their flank, breaking in and wreaking havoc. King Peter was amongst the dead and the slaughter was frightful. Simon and his crusaders believed they had God on their side; the besiegers were branded as heretical and as such could expect no quarter, and none was forthcoming. Muret was a remarkable victory and set the seal on Simon's already outstanding reputation. Sir Charles Oman describes the fight as a 'surprise' – indeed it was, for King Peter and his allies at least, but it indicates a level of tactical finesse and flexibility which is not often associated with battles of this era. Simon the son, sixth Earl of Leicester, was heir to that tradition: in his march to Lewes in 1264 and the deployment of his forces there is more than a distant echo of the earlier encounter.

It was the redoubtable William Marshal, Earl of Pembroke, who fought the only set-piece battle of the First Barons' War (1215–1217). The conflict was chiefly memorable for the epic sieges of Dover, Windsor and Rochester (see below). In May 1217 rebel magnates were before the walls of Lincoln: the castle was resolutely held by Nicola de Camville, served by a small but experienced garrison. The keep was on higher ground at the north-west apex of the town, with the streets sloping generally south toward the banks of the River Witham. William had mustered his relieving force at Newark, comprising some 400 knights, 300 hired crossbows and a substantial body of men-at-arms, the mercenaries under Fawkes de Breaute. On the night of 18 May the host encamped around Stow, some nine miles distant from their objective. Next morning they resumed their march, ascending to the high ground over which ran the old Roman highway of Ermine Street. Tactically this was sound, as the route provided a good approach to Lincoln and avoided the hazard of ambush – if the enemy chose to fight they must do so at some distance from the walls and either mask the garrison or risk a sortie in rear.

Each of the four divisions or battles was commanded by one of the royalist magnates: the earl of Chester took the van, Pembroke himself the main body, Salisbury the rear and Peter des Roches, fighting Bishop of Winchester, the reserve.[8] The continental bowmen were thrown forward as skirmishers. Such an array could not be concealed from the barons, whose scouts observed the royalists to be fewer in number and that an engagement on open ground was therefore to be preferred. However, when the commander of the French contingent came up to see for himself, he appears to have mistaken the royalists' baggage train for a further division and consequently counselled caution. To remain behind the town walls, whilst tactically passive, seemed to offer the rebels an inexpugnable position. William was now in a difficult tactical impasse: storming the town against superior numbers seemed impossible, and the besiegers, masked by the rest of the rebel defenders, could continue to concentrate on breaching the castle walls, with their engines already deployed.

One opportunity remained. In the western sector of the enceinte a handy postern was uncovered – through this the royalists could get their men into the castle and then prepare to sally out in force. This possibility had, of course, occurred to the barons, who assumed their forces before the walls adequate to repel any such initiative. An attack would have to be put in on a very constricted frontage, and the movement of troops beforehand would be both time-consuming and blindingly obvious. The royalists were left unmolested before the town walls to ponder what might best be done. John Marshal, Pembroke's nephew, made a dash for the postern and brought back news that matters within stood at a grave pass; consequently William dispatched the bishop to further reconnoitre, the cleric being noted for his sound tactical eye. He discovered that some potential might exist where the blocked-up west gate of the town – which had been abandoned because of its proximity to the north-west corner of the castle – stood unguarded. Bishop Peter found he could approach the old gateway from the castle without being detected; boldly he gave the garrison instructions that they should follow in his footsteps, and set a working party to break through the shoddy rubble blocking the arch. The bishop's plan was to send a commanded party into the castle and launch a sally; this would in fact be no more than a mere diversion, the main attack being put in through the uncovered gateway.

With his mercenary crossbowmen shooting from the castle walls and causing considerable discomfort to the besiegers below, the Marshal approached with the main body along the northern side of the city wall. The diversion was succeeding admirably, and de Breaute followed up his advantage with a bold sally. Although repulsed, and sustaining losses, the Frenchman's energy occupied the rebels' attention to the extent that the royalists were able to gain entry via the exposed gateway, and simultaneously their attacks upon the north and west gates broke in. John Marshal now took the besiegers in flank, relieving the pressure on their mercenary comrades and overrunning the engines. As his nephew did good work before the castle walls, William piled his men through the streets and a series of vicious melees, mostly fought rather surprisingly on horseback, erupted. The fighting, as might be expected in such narrow confines, was confused and protracted. Gradually the royalists pushed the enemy backwards toward the area around the cathedral and the south gate. Here the rebel Count of Perche attempted a rally which collapsed with his death; the rebels faltered, briefly steadied then broke, spilling southwards from the heaving streets. William the Marshal gained a famous victory and a rich haul of prisoners, including some 25 signatories of Magna Carta.[9]

The army

For such a war of rapid manoeuvre, mounted troops clearly held a considerable advantage. In the thirteenth century the standard tactical unit for cavalry ('the horse') was the ten-man conroi; this was favoured by the Knights Templar, though larger formations were also coming into fashion – twenty-man squadrons, latterly expanded into a unit comprising four bannerets, 16 knights and 80 squires. Following Templar practice the knight may have formed up with one of his attendants to bear the lance, a second in reserve at rear with spare horses and kit. As the squadron commenced its deployment the squire would hand his master the lance and follow on.

Those embarking on knightly service were customarily furnished with letters of protection. These were, in effect, legal indemnities providing immunity from adverse proceedings which might arise whilst the holder was on active service. The Holkham Picture Bible, produced some time later, in the early years of the fourteenth century, contains a pair of very striking images arranged one above the other. The uppermost shows a scene of savage combat, mailed knights in melee; the lower reveals infantry ('the foot') likewise engaged, in a furious if less gentlemanly fracas, swords, bucklers, axes and the fearsome falchion much in evidence.

Numbers could be quite significant: for the first of his Welsh campaigns Edward I recruited some 15,000 foot, many of whom were drawn from the southern fringes of the principality. For his later campaign against Wallace in 1298 the king mustered over 20,000 infantry. In subsequent campaigns these numbers were much reduced; poor societies could not support such large forces which would strip the land like locusts. A contemporary chronicler has left us an image of the English army on the march during the Scottish campaign of 1300:

> There were many rich caparisons embroidered on silks and satins; many a beautiful pennon fixed to a lance, many a banner displayed. The neighing of horses was heard from afar; the mountains and valleys were covered with pack-horses, tents and pavilions.[10]

Such a colourful vision, which could come directly from the pen of Scott or Tennyson, is highly idealized. The reality would be rather more mundane. Knights would ride light horses, palfreys, on the line of march, saving their precious destriers for combat. The armies would proceed in a cacophony of noise and dust, mounted arm to the front and as rearguard, mainly with harness stowed, horses throwing up vast clouds of muck; the foot tramped in long, straggling columns, ill-fed, ill-accoutred and swallowing the dust kicked up by their betters.

A vast caravanserai of livestock was required, for the army took its provisions along on the hoof, its wagons laden with small beer, tents, cordage, baggage and provisions. In the wake of the fighting men followed a horde of sutlers, tapsters, whores and tradesmen. The latter were an important element in the army's ability to function: armourers, sword-smiths, bowyers, fletchers, coopers, carpenters, surgeons and quack apothecaries, labourers, wheelwrights and herdsmen. Armies were not welcomed; locals would and with cause fear their passage, whether foe or nominal friend. People in the countryside lived an existence untrammelled by the vast and constant noise of the modern world: this great, resounding tramp of the army, its volume growing and receding like the ebb and flow of the tide across an otherwise quiet landscape, must have seemed like the very wrath of God. Where discipline was lax, rapine and pillage could spread like a contagion; the Anglo–Scottish wars which began from 1296 were characterized by a particular savagery that did not distinguish civil from military, and where harrying the populace became an accepted tactic of economic warfare.

Engaging in battle is and always has been a hazardous business. In the thirteenth century a commander had limited forces at his disposal, some perhaps of uncertain quality; a single defeat in the field could be catastrophic. Communications were dependent upon gallopers and, where possible, signalling with flags; supply and victualling were a constant headache. The army was habitually divided into four corps, each led by a person of magnatial rank; nobility were notoriously loath to take instruction from a social inferior (and not infrequently recalcitrant regardless of the status of the one giving orders).

When the king commanded the host then he would invariably lead one division, surrounded by his household men and with the corps commanders' term fixed only for the immediate duration. Once battle was joined the commander-in-chief could do little to influence the final outcome, his dispositions made and his forces committed. On the field, forces would deploy in linear formation, with opposing divisions aligned; generally there was little scope for complex manoeuvre before the advance to contact. Any good commander needs an eye for ground but the medieval general could not afford to have his reserves stationed too far distant lest, in the time it took them to come up, the day might already be lost.

A contemporary writer sums up the chivalric approach to the hazard of battle:

> What a joyous thing is war, for many fine deeds are seen in its course, and many good lessons learnt from it ... You love your comrade so much in war. When you see that your quarrel is just and your blood is fighting well, tears rise in your eyes. A great sweet feeling of loyalty and pity fills your heart on seeing your friend so valiantly exposing his body to execute and accomplish the command of our Creator. And then you prepare to go and live or die with him, and for love not abandon him. And out of that there arises such a delectation, that he who has not tasted it is not fit to say what a delight is. Do you think that a man who does that fears death? Not at all; for he feels strengthened, he is so elated, that he does not know where he is. Truly he is afraid of nothing.[11]

Good intelligence was, as ever, vital in the conduct of military operations. Edward I had knowledge of his enemy's dispositions before the raid on Kenilworth which he put to good effect and, when an army was operating in unfamiliar country, scouts, 'scourers' or 'prickers' were its eyes and ears. In the course of the Falkirk campaign Edward had been considering abandoning the advance and leading his hungry army, still unblooded, southwards. It was at this nadir that his scouts brought news of the Scottish army deployed nearby, intelligence which was to dramatically affect the outcome.

We should not forget that, despite the supposed influence of chivalry, 'frightfulness', the deliberate harrying of an enemy's lands and civilian population, was an accepted tactic: conquest by terror and waste. As a form of economic warfare this was undoubtedly effective, destroying the enemy's crops and indeed the tools needed to produce them. Such tactics also struck at the social order. Good 'lordship' was an essential element in the baron's relationship with his tenants; if this was damaged or destroyed the lord's position became increasingly tenuous. Plunder was a prime incentive for medieval soldiers, and such robbery also reduced the fiscal wealth of the enemy. Jean II, King of France, after signing the humiliating Treaty of Brétigny in 1360, explained his willingness to agree to such terms in the following manner:

> Because of the said wars many mortal battles have been fought, people slaughtered, churches pillaged, bodies destroyed and souls lost, maids and virgins deflowered, respectable wives and widows dishonoured, towns, manors and buildings burnt and robberies, oppressions and ambushes on the roads and highways committed. Justice has failed because of them, the Christian faith has chilled and commerce has perished, and so many other evils and horrible deeds have followed from these wars that they cannot be said, numbered or written.[12]

Arms and armour
In Simon de Montfort's day the mounted knight relied mainly upon chain mail for bodily defence, together with a flat-topped helmet with narrow eye-slits ('the sights'), cheek pieces perforated for limited ventilation, with arming cap and a mail hood or 'coif' worn underneath. His mail would consist of two garments: a long-sleeved thigh-length shirt called a hauberk, and leg defences or hosen (chause). Mail is both flexible and, when compared with plate, quite light. However, it may not protect the wearer against a crushing blow, which can cause severe contusions or fractures even if the links hold. That vulnerable area around the neck received extra protection from a stiff laced collar, a form of

gorget, and possibly reinforced with steel plates. Occasionally the coat of plates (a descendant of the *lorica squamata* of the classical age) was preferred; mailed gauntlets or mittens were carried to protect the hands. By the dawn of the fourteenth century the thighs were further protected by tubed defences worn over mail and linking to knee guards or poleyns.

As the need for greater protection grew it became commonplace, following continental fashion, for the horseman to secure additional protection in the form of a poncho-like garment reinforced with steel plates to back and breast. Shoulder defences or ailettes were also added, often bearing the wearer's heraldic device. Shields, shaped like the base of an iron and curved to conform with the contours of the body, were also still carried. The increasing use of the longbow after 1300 spurred the need for further improvements – mail could not resist the deadly bodkin point, and gutter-shaped plate defences to the arms and legs were introduced, strapped on over the mail.

For the knight, aside from his harness his biggest investment was in his war horse or destrier (*dextrarius*), which would probably cost around £40, a sizeable sum, equal to twice the basic property qualification for knight service. Good bloodstock came from France, Spain and Hungary: a sound horse could cost up to £30. The animals were not as large as modern hunters, typically between 15 and 16 hands but with good, strong legs, deep chest and broad back. As a rule the destrier was reserved for the charge; on the line of march the knight would ride the lesser palfrey, whilst his followers jogged along behind on inexpensive rouncies.[13]

With its high bow and cantle the knightly saddle provided both additional protection against slashing cuts and also gave support which, coupled with the use of the stirrups, gave the knight the necessary platform for combat. The valuable war horse was itself to a degree armoured, with two sections of protective covering, before and behind the saddle. The fore part covered the head, with openings for nose, eyes and mouth; the longer rear portion reached as far as the hocks. This leather and quilted harness was stiffened by the chamfron, a plate section shaped to the horse's face –

striking at the face was a standard footman's tactic. As he prepared himself for combat the knight would keep his lance in an upright position. The lighter spear-like weapon of the Conquest era had given way to a stouter, heavier model that was carried in the couched position under the arm, held securely against the rider's flank and angled to the left over the neck of his mount, resting on the shield. The amount of movement was circumscribed: a wider arc could be created only by 'aiming' the horse.

When the horse trotted forward, approaching the canter, the rider would lift the lance clear of the rest and wedge his buttocks firmly against the cantle, leaning forward with his knees fixed, something like a modern jockey. In this position the shock of impact, which could otherwise result in an ignominious and potentially fatal tumble, was dispersed from the shoulders, through the rider's chest and buttocks onto the solid bulk of the mount. The position also favoured the use of the sword, once the lance, essentially a 'one-shot' weapon, was expended. In terms of its symbolic potency the sword was the very emblem of knightly rank, its blade imbued with the legendary spirit of Excalibur. By the early fourteenth century the knightly sword was a long-bladed, predominantly single-handed blade, double-edged with a broad, straight, full-length fuller. Hand-and-a-half swords, 'swords of war', had longer blades (there is a record from Longshanks' day of a sword from Cologne with a blade length of 45 inches and a 5 inch hilt). Quillons were long and either straight or turned up toward the point.

Daggers were a preferred accessory, fashioned like miniature swords and intended for stabbing; it was standard practice to dispatch an armoured foe, once brought to the ground, with the point of the knife driven in through the sights of the helmet or into armpit or groin as the *coup de grâce*. The commons might carry the heavy broad-bladed falchion, a cleaver-like weapon, which could deliver a cut of tremendous force. A very fine example, the Conyers Falchion, survives in Durham Cathedral. Danish axes, for the infantry, mounted on 6 foot shafts, were still very much in evidence; mounted warriors might use the shorter horseman's axe or a mace.

Although it is unlikely the cavalry charge ever reached the speeds represented by Hollywood knights on film, probably never faster than a moderate canter, the sight of these caparisoned horsemen, grimly anonymous in their crested helms, their lance points bristling, a ton and more of mailed rider and horse bearing down inexorably, would be terrifying, particularly to raw foot. Once tumbled from his horse, however, the knight forfeited his apparent invulnerability. William the Lion, surprised before the leaguer of Alnwick in 1174, boldly charged his mounted opponents and unhorsed one, but when his horse was then killed beneath him he was hopelessly pinned beneath the carcass. A generation earlier the fearsome Richard Marshal, son of the famous William, Earl of Pembroke, a lion in the melee, hacked both hands from one attacker who sought to grapple him, fighting off all challengers till unhorsed and swiftly brought down by common foot-soldiers, sustaining injuries that proved mortal.[14]

Whilst knights and men-at-arms would wear full harness, archers tended to favour padded 'jacks' or 'brigandines'. These were fabric garments reinforced with plates of steel or bone riveted to the leather or canvas, sometimes just stuffed with rags. Much lighter and cheaper than plate, these afforded surprisingly good protection and were sometimes finished with sleeves of mail. Though archers generally did not wear leg protection, billmen and men-at-arms might wear full- or part-leg harness. By this time the crude peasants' bill had been refined into an elegant killing implement, with a long head tapering to a point, the blade furnished with a hook and a handy spike on the back edge. When the bill and spear collided, the latter had the edge in length, but when momentum was lost the bill could quickly develop the upper hand in a melee. Billmen, like their more esteemed contemporaries, the archers, practised long and hard with their weapon, and the English became renowned in its use. In close combat the axe blade could lop the head off the spear, unless, as was rarely the case, the point was fitted with steel strips or languets. Then the holder was left with a rather unwieldy stick. Perhaps the most famous instance of a mass duel of this nature occurred in the course of the much later Battle of Flodden in 1513, when the

Scottish pike formations, having lost cohesion in a disorderly advance, were bested by English bills.

Yew was the timber most favoured by bowyers, though ash, elm and wych elm were also employed. The stave was around six feet in length, in section akin to a rounded 'D'. An average draw weight might be anywhere from 80 to 120lb (as a comparison, a modern sporting bow has a pull of about 45lb). Momentum, defined as mass multiplied by velocity, was considerable, and the stout yeomen of England could, it was said, punch a hardened bodkin point through several inches of oak at distances of up to 200 yards. Mail was not sure protection, and the lesser harnessed foot would suffer terribly. The damage wrought upon Wallace's spears at Falkirk is ample testimony to the killing power of the bow when deployed in massed formation.

Arrows were made from a variety of woods. Roger Ascham, Elizabeth I's tutor and a noted authority from the much later sixteenth century, advocated aspen as the most suitable, though ash, alder, elder, birch, willow and hornbeam were also utilized. The shafts were generally around 2 feet 6 inches in length, the fletching made from grey goose feathers. Arrowheads came in a variety of forms: flat, hammer-headed, barbed, wickedly sharp needle points or bodkins to punch through plate. Arrows were described as 'livery' (being issued to retainers), 'standard' (made to a universal specification) and 'sheaf' (as they came in bundles of 24).

The bow was tipped at each end with cow-horn, grooved to take the linen string; when not in use the stave was carried, unstrung, in a cloth bag. To draw, the archer gripped the bow with his left hand about the middle, where the circumference was around four and a half inches, then he forced the centre of the bow away from him to complete the draw, using the weight of his body to assist rather than relying on the strength in his arms alone. Such expertise required constant training, and practice at the butts was compelled by statute. Long-range shooting was preferred, and the bow was effective at over 200 yards, a distinct advantage over the later matchlock musket, which was seldom effective beyond 50 paces. A leather or horn 'bracer' was strapped to the wrist to protect the archer from the snap of the bowstring.

Siege warfare

Warfare was for centuries dominated by the perpetual and symbiotic duel between those who sought to erect defences and those who sought the means to knock them down. This contest continued until the age of gunpowder profoundly altered the balance; prior to that the advantage typically lay with the defender.

It was the Normans, with their timber motte and bailey fortifications, who truly introduced the castle into England. During the twelfth century timber was gradually replaced by masonry; great stone keeps, such as Rochester, Orford, Conisburgh, Richmond and Newcastle, soared mightily. The castle was not just a fort: it was the lord's residence, the seat and symbol of his power, centre of his administration, a secure base from which his mailed household could hold down a swathe of territory. Castles were both potent and symbolic: the civil wars of Stephen and Matilda had spawned a pestilence of unlicensed building, fuelling the magnatial threat to crown authority. Castles grew thickest on the disputed marches of England, facing the Welsh and Scots; in the north-west the mighty red sandstone fortress of Carlisle stood resolute, to the Scots who coveted Cumberland a clear statement, as George MacDonald Fraser pithily put it: 'sod off in stone.'

Concentric castles, influenced by Arab and Byzantine precedent, appeared when Edward I, as king, began his great chain of towering Welsh fortresses; during the earlier thirteenth century there had been little technical advance. As the country had enjoyed a long spell of peace many lords had invested in what might now be termed 'makeovers' – aiming to improve standards of living rather than adding to defences. Larger, more ornate chapels and fine great halls replaced their workaday predecessors; gardens and orchards were laid out to provide tranquil spaces within the enceinte. Most castles of the period relied upon the strength of the great keep: tall, massive, towering in fine ashlar with the lower vaulted basement reserved for storage and an entrance at first-floor level, frequently now enclosed in a defensive fore-building. On this level we would typically find the great hall with a chapel and the lord's private apartment or solar on the second floor above. Spirals were set in the thickness of the wall leading to a rooftop parapet walk, often with corner towers. The enceinte was girded by a strong stone wall enclosing the courtyard or bailey, which would also house the usual domestic offices. The keep was essentially a refuge, a passive defence.

From the reign of Henry II onward, strong flanking towers were frequently added to provide defence against mining. The polygonal keep at Orford in Suffolk (1165–1173) is a fine example; at Pembroke, William the Marshal built an entirely circular keep. The curtain wall was also raised and strengthened, furnished with D-shaped towers, the section beyond the curtain rounded at the corners to frustrate mining. These towers made the attacker's job much more difficult. If he breached or surmounted a section of the rampart, he would be corralled between the towers which would now have to be assaulted in turn. This was leading toward the concentric design where the strength of the enceinte was distributed through the towers, and the great keep, as a feature, became redundant.

Traditional siege engines, whose design remained unchanged from classical times, the ballista and the mangonel dominated siege warfare during the thirteenth century – cannon and the devil's roar were yet to make their appearance. The ballista was, in effect, a giant crossbow which hurled a bolt or occasionally stones at the enemy's ramparts. It was intended as an anti-personnel weapon, flensing unwary defenders from the walls, used to cover an assault or escalade. Chief amongst engines was the mighty trebuchet, most probably Arab in origin. This worked by counterpoise in that the device was built with a timber beam which was pivoted between two sturdy posts; one end of the beam had ropes affixed and the sling was fitted to the other. Initially, when the ball was loaded into the sling, a group of hefty infantry simply hauled on the ropes, pivoting upwards the shorter end of the timber, and the sling at the ready moment released the projectile.

Latterly, a large counterweight, a timber-framed box casing filled with soil or rubble, supplanted raw muscle; by now the machines were much larger and the box might weigh anything over 10,000lb.[15] These trebuchets grew to considerable proportions and consumed much wood in their building. Missiles, which might weigh 100–200lb or more, were flung at a high trajectory, like the shell from a later howitzer. Thus the internal spaces of the castle could be deluged in a rain of stones which, shattering on impact, would send lethal shards whizzing like shrapnel. The bombardment thus assumed something of the aspect of the artillery barrage, deadly and relentless, the defenders clinging to shelter whilst it endured.

When the castellan became aware that a leaguer was imminent it was time to prepare. Supply was a major concern: clearly adequate foodstuffs and a clean water supply were essential to maintain the garrison for what might stretch to several months of encirclement. Sheep, cattle and livestock would be gathered in, the surrounding countryside stripped to deny the attacker. Ditches would be cleared and consolidated, repairs to the masonry undertaken, trees, bushes and inconvenient settlements would be demolished or thoroughly slighted so as to deny cover to the enemy. Timber hoardings, called brattices, would be erected over the parapet walk to provide a covered fighting platform; the defenders' own artillery serviced, repaired as necessary and made ready supplies of missiles and arrows brought in.

Siege warfare was costly, time-consuming and tedious. The attacker might languish before the ramparts for long and frustrating weeks, consuming his supplies at a fearsome rate, at risk from the defenders' sallies, from dysentery in the crowded lines or from a relieving force. He would try to negotiate; to persuade the castellan to come to terms; if he acceded before the lines were fixed then convention would allow the defenders to march out under arms and depart unmolested. If cajolery failed, then threats might suffice; in this captives were useful tools. In 1139 King Stephen persuaded the mother of Roger le Poer to surrender Devizes or see her son hanged before the walls. Edward III, in 1333, when before the walls of Berwick, threatened to hang the governor's two young sons if the place did not open its gates: he refused and had to endure the agony of watching the wretched youths dance at ropes' end.

As the leaguer drew on, mercy shrank accordingly. If the place fell to storm then the attacker could put all within to the sword; offers of clemency once extended might not be repeated. Where the defenders, finding themselves in straits, subsequently sued for terms they might find the besieger less amenable. Even when a commander was disposed to magnanimity, his soldiery, deprived of spoil, might be disinclined to take heed. A civil war was, of course, a different matter: kings and magnates would not wish to see domestic towns and castles given over to sack unless, as in the case of the notorious siege and storming of Beziers in July 1209 during the suppression of the Cathars, the whiff of heresy was sufficient for the French knights breaking in to slaughter all, heretics and believers alike. The papal legate Arnaud Amaury is said to have quipped 'Kill them all. God will know his own.'[16]

Morale was a vital factor, as loss of nerve or resolution on the besiegers' part or the effect of exhaustion and despair could swiftly erode the garrison's will to resist. When laying siege to Stirling in 1304 Edward I refused to allow the defenders to formally surrender; the king had caused his engineers to build a giant trebuchet, the 'Warwolf', and he was anxious to test its effect. Siege warfare was attritional and brutal. Henry V, in the fifteenth century, refused to allow French civilians, expelled by the garrison commanders as *bouches inutiles*,[17] to pass through the lines; they became trapped in the bleak no-man's-land, left there to squat in filth and famine whilst the siege continued. Disease was a spectre that stalked both sides, especially during hot summer weather, yet it was extremely difficult to maintain a siege during stark and freezing winter.

In terms of tactics, storming or escalade was the quickest method of subduing a garrison but one fraught with peril, wherein the attacker stood to sustain significant loss. Edward I stormed the rather makeshift defences of Berwick upon Tweed in 1296: his veteran knights, hardened during the Welsh Wars, broke in and the town was given over to a bloody sack. Such instances were relatively rare and it was far more common for the attacker to seek to starve the garrison out. This entailed less tactical risk but was time-consuming and expensive; the besieger had to plan and fortify his camp, make it proof against sallies, stockpile his supplies, provide tents or bothies for his men and attempt some basic form of temporary sanitation. To be effective the blockade had to seal off the besieged completely from resupply. When throwing his great ring of concentric castles around the conquered principality Edward sited these so that, in the main, they could be resupplied from the sea. If the defenders could receive fresh supplies then the besiegers' task was made considerably more difficult.

Surprise and subterfuge were naturally at a premium. After the death of Edward I his son and successor lacked the fire to maintain the war against Bruce in Scotland. The latter steadily clawed back vital bastions, several of which were won by *coup de main* as the Scots lacked both the resources and engineering skills demanded of the conventional besieger. Treachery was a component, if the attacker could cultivate or suborn a faction within the walls; some form of Trojan Horse type duplicity might succeed where leaguer and escalade did not. To conduct a full-scale siege of an enemy stronghold then was likely to be a long-term and static affair, tying down the attacker's army or certainly large portions of it and robbing him of the strategic initiative. Conversely, simply to bypass the enemy stronghold was to leave a potential foe in rear which could emerge to harass and disrupt. As an alternative the fortress could be masked by a force sufficient for the task, simply to neutralize the defenders whilst the main attacking force remained fluid in the field.

Frightfulness was another tactic available to the attacker: he could frighten the besieged into surrender by wreaking havoc on his lands about. In 1123 Henry I 'took up' all the space around Pont-Audemer for a good 20 miles or so. Contemporary writers confirm that the army's scouts or prickers also acted as incendiaries and foragers, seizing what the army might use, destroying all else. Again, these tactics were limited during civil strife – what king wishes, if he can avoid it, to waste his own lands;

his quarrel is generally with individual magnates rather than necessarily with their wider affinity.

Where the attacking general had determined upon an assault to carry the walls, he would send in his attacking troops, chosen men, who would attempt to lay ladders against the ramparts; archers, protected by timber hoardings or pavises, would unleash a missile storm intended to keep the defenders' heads down. For their part the castellan's men would rely on their own bows and on a range of missiles to smash the ladders, massing to deal with those who gained the parapet, a desperate and bloody business. If a castle was protected by a strong water defence which prevented attempts at mining then the attacker might seek to assail the base of the walls with a ram or screw, manoeuvred over the moat after a pontoon of fascines (bundles of sticks or faggots) had been laid. The ram would be a solid baulk of timber housed in a wheeled shed which would offer the crew some protection; the beam was slung on ropes from the roof, swung to and fro to gather momentum. The screw was used to bore rather than batter; defenders would lower large hooks to catch and fling aside or drop great boulders to smash the protective carapace and crush its occupants. The belfry was a movable timber tower, higher at its upper level than the wall, and providing a platform for archers whilst infantry assaulted across a drawbridge; like all wooden devices these monsters were difficult to move, vulnerable to fire and involved a great deal of effort in their construction.

Mining had an ancient provenance, Joshua before the great walls of Jericho; it was a difficult and, for the miner, dangerous business. A shaft was sunk to carry under a corner of the great tower, with a chamber excavated directly underneath; this was supported by timber props, the whole crammed with combustible material and then fired to collapse a section of wall. Naturally military architects would endeavour to frustrate the miners' efforts by siting the castle on a foundation of solid rock or by providing water defences. The base of the wall could be splayed or 'battered' to provide a more formidable obstacle. The miner had to conceal the entry to his shaft so as to avoid alerting the defenders; dead ground or buildings could provide ideal cover. As an alternative to bringing down a section of wall the shaft could continue into the bailey, like the reverse of a Second World War escape tunnel, to enable the besiegers to launch a surprise attack and seize the gates. A prudent castellan might place buckets of water on the ramparts to detect tremors. If the wall was breached then the defenders would attempt to plug the gap with timbers or construct temporary screen walls. The more enterprising, on detecting mining against the walls, might attempt to sink a countermine; the object was to break into the attackers' shaft and engage the miners in a desperate and savage subterranean melee. Readers of Sebastian Faulks's highly accomplished Great War novel *Birdsong* will recall how these tactics were still employed on the Western Front, 1914-1918.

One of the most celebrated sieges of the era was the leaguer of Rochester by King John in autumn 1216. The king was advancing from Dover to London and, though he had previously installed a royal garrison, the castle had been handed to the Archbishop of Canterbury and was now held by a castellan, William de Albini, of the rebel faction. On 11 October the siege began in earnest, with the king sailing fireships[18] against the bridge spanning the Medway, across which any reinforcements would arrive. A sally was, with some difficulty, beaten back – John sacked and slighted the cathedral, a spiteful reminder to Archbishop Langton. Engines were constructed and mining operations opened a breach in the curtain; by early November the royalists had taken the bailey.

Further mines were dug under the south-east tower of the great keep; John had demanded two score of well-fleshed pigs who, having fed the army, continued their duty with their fat being used to fire the timbers supporting the mine cavern. Despite this reverse, the rebels clung to a portion of the keep; the great tower was divided by a strong internal partition that effectively created two defensible zones. Those who had surrendered were savagely mutilated to reflect the king's frustration. It was only on 30 November that the ravenous survivors capitulated; the patriotic swine were awarded their own memorial, and the garrison were lucky to escape with their lives.[19]

Only one commoner who had defected from royal service went to the gallows, the rest being sent to various gaols. The siege had cost the king a considerable sum, in the region of £1,000 per day, a prodigious outlay to subdue a rebel company of under 100 men-at-arms. Thus not only were sieges protracted, they entailed a huge drain on the attackers' resources. At the time Rochester's leaguer was viewed as something of an epic on account of the valour, fury and dogged persistence shown by both sides.

Naval actions certainly took place at this time. The merchantman of the day, only twice as long as it was broad, fat-bellied, slow to steer with fixed square mainsail, was the jack of all trades. For the conversion to man-of-war, timber 'castles' were fitted fore and aft. Tactics were usually restricted to grappling and boarding, missile power being provided by archers. Even ramming was near impossible and just as perilous for the aggressor. It was not until the fifteenth century that the earlier medieval vessel the 'cog', which had been fitted with a steering oar, was replaced by the more sophisticated 'nef' steered by rudder. By the thirteenth century the use of crossbows as on-board missile weapons was commonplace in the Mediterranean, whilst regular contingents of retained marines were also in evidence. However, both these trends were slower to catch on in northern waters. As fleets engaged, with limited manoeuvring, lime was used to blind opponents and soap was employed to render the enemy's decks slippery and treacherous underfoot; thereafter it was a case of grapple and board.

The face of battle

Time and much romantic fiction have cast a shroud of pageantry over the harsh realities of medieval combat, but the truth is somewhat less comforting. Though lacking the scale and devastation of modern wars, devoid of the horrors of machine guns and high explosive, warfare in the middle ages was every bit as frightful. Commanders might, as Bruce did, seek to exhort their men through inspiring oratory, though this is probably much exaggerated by chroniclers, as a general, even if he rode up and down the line, would be heard by only a small proportion at any one time. Morale was, as ever in war, paramount, as the Scots demonstrated at Myton and other skirmishes after Bannockburn, where their discipline, cohesion and faith in their officers created in their forces a formidable instrument of war. The knight had his years of training, pride in his lineage, the scorn and excoriation of his peers should he waver to sustain him; the commons had less, much less. Faith too was important: the thirteenth century was an age when it was paramount. Christendom had yet to be rent by the fires of schism. The early heretics the Bogomils and Cathars had been ruthlessly and effectively suppressed.[20] However cynically men might act, this did not affect the integrity of their belief: battle was seen as a manifestation of God's divine will, and hearing mass and taking the sacrament were considered imperatives to a man embarking on the hazard of combat.

Our present age, mired in arid secularism, has lost the compelling nature of medieval religiosity, but the validity and importance of faith should not be overlooked. Clerics, though banned from bearing arms, were frequently to be seen in harness: Anthony Bek, the prince bishop who held office from 1283, was till his death in 1311 a significant leader in war.[21] Once battle was joined in earnest the combat became an intensely personal affair, a hacking, stamping melee of bills, spears, sword and axe. Men, half blind in armour, soon assailed by raging thirst and fatigue, would swiftly become disorientated. Few would be killed by a single blow, but a disabling wound, bringing the victim to ground, would expose him to more and fatal blows, most likely to the head or the dagger thrust through the visor, a horrible, agonizing and by no means speedy end.

Images from the period show appalling injuries as helmets are split and men riven to the navel. Modern tests have shown a stout steel skull will resist a shearing blow; nonetheless the carnage at close quarters will have been utterly horrifying. Many men died not from blows but from suffocation in the press, as at Dupplin Moor in 1332, or by drowning as they sought to flee over watercourses – hundreds of English corpses clogged the Bannockburn and the Swale at Myton five years later. A battle could be divided into a number of phases: it might commence with an archery duel, with the side that came off worse being forced to advance to contact; the horse would then advance and engage with their opposite numbers or, as at Falkirk and Bannockburn, assault the enemy spears. When one side broke, dissolving in rout, then the pursuit might be both long and bloody. Men who had staunchly held their ground would give way to the contagion of panic, casting aside arms and harness – easy meat.

These horrors were repeated on many fields in the Scottish wars, Halidon Hill and Homildon being just two examples. It must also be borne in mind that knights in particular were professional fighting men, physically hardy and tremendously fit, reckoned to be easily the equal in prowess and stamina of today's special forces.[22] A fourteenth-century work describes how the bravado of the man-at-arms rapidly diminishes the closer to contact he comes:

> When we are in taverns, drinking strong wines, at our sides the ladies we desire, looking on, with their smooth throats ... . Their grey eyes shining back with smiling beauty nature calls on us to have desiring hearts, to struggle awaiting [their] thanks at the end. That we would conquer ... Oliver and Roland; but when we are in the field, on our galloping chargers our shields round our necks and lances lowered ... and our enemies are approaching us then we would rather be deep in some cavern.[23]

By modern standards medical services were rudimentary and unreliable. The perceived presence of evil humours was the source of much bleeding of patients; quacks cast horoscopes and prescribed bizarre potions; wounds were cauterized with hot pitch. However, the use of forms of anaesthesia, derived mainly from herbs, was not unknown, and surgical techniques were perhaps more advanced, at least in the hands of competent practitioners, than may be imagined. One of the dead from Towton recently exhumed from a grave pit on the site (1996) showed evidence of a prior and massive facial injury which had been skilfully repaired. Nonetheless throughout the period northern European medical services lagged far behind those available both to Byzantine and to Islamic armies.

As we have seen, most fatal injuries were caused by blows to the head, as the mute remains from grave pits testify – at Otterburn the bodies of the English dead, whose remains were found beneath the nave of Elsdon church in the nineteenth century, at Visby in Sweden (1361) and at Towton. Slashing and stabbing wounds, though ghastly, were not always fatal and more victims probably recovered than might be expected. Complications such as peritonitis or blood poisoning, however, were invariably fatal – many injured would be left lying on the field exposed to the rigours of climate and the tender mercies of scavengers. Campaigns of the period tended to be highly mobile and of relatively short duration. War was primarily a specialized activity, carried on by seasoned practitioners.

This then was the state of the art of war in the second half of the thirteenth century, an era where the mailed horseman still dominated the field, when much blood and treasure was expended in besieging strongholds, when chivalry was still the code of the warrior-gentleman. Strategy, in the modern sense, is perceived to be lacking but this is overly simplistic – Prince Edward demonstrated at Evesham a fine grasp of strategic principles and a developing mastery of tactics that was to lead to his important victory over the Scots under Wallace at Falkirk in 1298. This was an early example of the successful and practised deployment of combined arms, archers and cavalry – the first employed to destroy the static ranks of enemy spear formations, the latter to chase the inferior Scottish horse, to overrun his own archers and finally to exploit the gaps in the spears opened by the arrow storm. De Montfort, had he lived, might have had cause to be proud of his pupil.

Chapter 2

The Reign of Henry III

O n a warm summer's day in 1265, rather more than warm, where a fierce electrical storm added a Wagnerian flourish to the high drama being enacted just outside the town of Evesham, Henry III of England found himself a helpless spectator to the furious battle being fought for control of his kingdom. The puppet of the baronial faction, he had been led to the field in full harness and now wandered, impotent and largely irrelevant, as the violent denouement of the Second Barons' War flared around him – 'I am Henry of Winchester your king, do not kill me!'[1] Wounded in the shoulder and in peril of being cut down in the frenzy, he was finally rescued by his eldest son; as a contribution to the restoration of his authority, the king's role on the field was something below inspirational.

The nature of kingship

Kings and kingship were the foundation of English polity in the medieval period. The king stood at the head of the social and economic pyramid, supported by a sophisticated legal and fiscal framework that had evolved steadily since the Conquest. The king was responsible for maintaining law and order at home and for securing the realm against external threat. A successful monarch, such as Henry II or Edward I, needed to work closely with his leading magnates; they represented the landed interest, and ownership of land was all-important. Since Magna Carta and the important constitutional reforms taking place during Henry III's reign the king's conduct was held to be subject to the law – a king such as Henry himself who sought to rule arbitrarily could forfeit the obedience of the magnates; the king's rule might be ordained by God but this did not excuse or exonerate tyranny.

Should the king, however, behave in an authoritarian and unjust manner, he remained king; the subject owed him an absolute duty of obedience. In such an instance, which had arisen during the rule of King John, and latterly that of his son, there was no certainty about what should be done to bring the monarch to account. His removal was contrary to God's law: usurpation was a crime against the laws of man and of God. That the kings of England were frequently at war with external enemies, in Wales, Ireland, Scotland and France, gave rise to the reality of taxation – a constitutional acceptance that the burden of these conflicts should be borne collectively. The process was by no means swift or absolutely certain: not until the reign of Edward III was there a general acceptance that the sovereign had the right to levy tax, due as a portion of the individual subject's wealth, and then legitimized by Act of Parliament. Royal finances were complex but essentially revolved around the concepts of 'ordinary' revenue, which the king derived from customs revenues plus the income from his estates, and 'extraordinary' revenue, which was voted as a tax. The former was expected to cover his normal household and administrative expenses, the latter to extend to defence of the realm, frequently and in practice implying armed expeditions abroad.

By far the most influential class, in political terms, were the magnates, the great landowners; not only did they control vast acres but they provided the military 'muscle' which the crown needed to enforce its will. There was no standing army as such: the magnates with their household men and retainers formed the nucleus of any military force the monarch needed, either to deal with civil discord or to fight abroad. Through the web of nobility controlling and scattered throughout the shires the king could exercise control over the whole and raise forces for his campaigns. Throughout the high medieval period the nobility, if unchecked, had a tendency to settle their disputes by force of arms, particularly the prickly marcher lords who, as frontiersmen, were frequently in the field. The plain fact was that the administrative authority of the king, in terms of available force, was upheld by privately raised contingents which he did not directly control. A twenty-first century analogy would be the delegation in Iraq of internal security to private contractors, security firms that are themselves the direct employers of the local forces involved.

To be successful the king needed to be accessible and receptive. His status might be conferred by God but the magnates were not overly deferential; most had opinions and were forthright in expressing them. Even authoritarian figures such as Edward I faced magnatial opposition: peers such as the earls of Norfolk and Hereford were not cowed by royal rages, impressive and volcanic as these were. When Henry III chose to ride roughshod over the advice and privileges of the magnates, he invited stern opposition. As a class the nobility were generally well educated, experienced and skilful in the management of their estates, and frequently well versed in war, the gentleman's trade.

Simon de Montfort was just such a nobleman, and we shall consider his character and achievement below. If the authority of the crown was very considerable then the obligation to use its powers both wisely and justly was implicit. When the royal authority was weakened then internal discord could fester and foreign enemies strike; the strife that erupted at the end of King John's reign is a case in point. What then to do with a king whose despotic incompetence proved intolerable? John and his son Henry III were neither of them deposed, but a form of constitutional settlement was forced upon them which, in both instances, sparked outbreaks of civil war.

The First Barons' War (1215–1217) and the early years of Henry III

Henry III was in some respects fortunate in that he came to the throne at a time when economic conditions were improving. The population, which stood at around 2,500,000 souls by the end of the thirteenth century, had roughly doubled since 1066. Though England was still a mainly rural economy, the development of trade and increases in the number of inhabitants had spurred urban growth; improvements in agriculture, such as crop rotation, ensured the land could feed a swelling populace. Fat sheep grazing on downland and pasture provided, with their wool, a basis for prosperity; technological innovations linked to the increasing harnessing of wind power and the move from a purely supply-based economy to one which exported finished goods fuelled growth.

The king had come to the throne young, a mere nine years of age when his father, King John 'Lackland', died, unlamented by most. John has not enjoyed a good press. His reign began in the spring of 1199, opening in a dangerous struggle with his nephew Arthur,[2] whose bid was supported by Philip II of France. The feud was resolved by treaty with France which confirmed the king in his French holdings, but a subsequent dispute over John's proposed marriage to Isabella of Angouleme[3] resulted in forfeiture of Normandy and all the Angevin lands save Gascony. In the subsequent fighting Arthur was captured and certainly killed; some alleged that the lad died by the king's own hand. True or not, John gained a reputation for ruthlessness. His troubles were then compounded by a damaging dispute with the papacy, which resulted in an interdict and excommunication. Though successful in his Welsh campaign of 1211 he was badly beaten three years later at Bouvines by the French. The defeat exacerbated tensions with his leading magnates who, on 15 June 1215, at Runnymede, compelled him to agree the terms of Magna Carta. This unprecedented restriction on the royal prerogative proved unpalatable, and the dispute between king and magnates quickly degenerated into the First Barons' War.

Constitutional matters were soon sidelined during what developed into a dynastic struggle; the rebel barons, so disgusted with John, invited the French Prince Louis to take the throne. Despite misgivings from both father and pope, the prince at first sent men then launched an expedition, making landfall in Kent on 22 May 1216. John fell back and allowed the French to occupy his capital. A slew of magnates, including the King of Scotland, hastened to acknowledge Louis's claim, prompting further defections from the king's faction. Winchester fell, but then the invaders sat down before the redoubtable walls of Dover, as ever the key to the kingdom. An epic siege, lasting three months, then began, but the attackers could make no serious headway, and by October Louis was glad to call a truce. Windsor also held out, but the most famous leaguer, as described above, was John's siege of Rochester.

King John died, embittered and broken, at Newark on 18 or 19 October 1216. The accession of the nine-year-old Henry changed the complexion of the civil war, with the barometer of baronial support swinging away from Louis in favour of the boy king. As the French still held London he had to be crowned in Gloucester Abbey, on 28 October. William Marshal, the great Earl of Pembroke, the very epitome of chivalry and acting as guardian, signed an amended draft of Magna Carta. With such a renowned knight to argue his cause and the Charter agreed, it was Louis's turn to suffer a rash of defections, though the war spluttered on for months. Dover was again besieged but the king's faction won the important fight at Lincoln (see above) and the French suffered signal reverses at sea. Finally, the French prince was obliged to concede defeat, and terms were agreed by the Treaty of Lambeth entered into on 11 September 1217.

Trevet described Henry III in maturity as being of a stocky build, medium height and narrow forehead; a distinctive feature was his drooping left eyelid.[4] Noted, even in an age of ostentatious piety, for his rigorous, perhaps even excessive devotion, often attending mass several times during the day, he was a very public devotee of the cult of Edward the Confessor, canonized in 1161. It was this fixation which prompted him not only to name his eldest son after the saint but also to fix Westminster Hall as the seat of government.[5] He was a noted patron of the arts, particularly architecture, and he engaged French craftsmen from Rheims to refurbish Westminster Abbey, a process that continued for several decades with his great shrine to the Confessor not being completed till 1269. As he championed Christ so did he persecute Jews; in expressing pronounced anti-Semitism he was by no means alone in an age which dealt harshly with Jewry. Henry enacted a series of anti-Jewish policies, including the mandatory requirement for followers of Judaism to wear the distinguishing symbol of the Two Tablets, a 'badge of shame'.[6] Henry has been described as 'a warm hearted man, quick to anger, but also quick to forgive, loving, generous, accessible and amiable . . . As numerous contemporaries complained he was a *vir simplex* – a naïve man'.[7]

On 14 January 1236 Henry married Eleanor of Provence, the daughter of Ramon Berenguer IV, Count of Toulouse, and Beatrice of Savoy, a noted beauty – though, if Matthew Paris is to be believed, no more than 12 years old when she came to England. She would bear the king five children: Edward, the eldest and probably her favourite, would become one of the most successful of English medieval sovereigns. His sister Margaret was wed to Alexander III of Scotland; his untimely death in 1286 would, in due course, prompt Longshanks' meddling in Scottish affairs, and, after 1296, usher in the 'Three Hundred Years War' with Scotland. Eleanor was capable and confidant, and in her train she imported a gaggle of acquisitive relations, collectively known as the Savoyards: these incomers did not find favour with the English polity, swelling the magnates' resentment of 'foreigners' – a level of xenophobia that was significantly compounded by another immigrant group, the Lusignans.

John's widow Isabella of Angouleme had, as her second husband, Hugh X of Lusignan, Count of La Marche; her sons by this union, William de Valence, Aymer de Valence and Guy de Lusignan, were thus King Henry's half-brothers. When the French occupied Poitou after 1246, this placed the Lusignans in difficulties, and Henry permitted them to cross the Channel in the next year. The king did very well by his half-siblings. William was married to Joan de Munchensy, from whom he received a portion of the Marshal estates. He was aggressive in his own advancement and not overly troubled by notions of due process; he swiftly alienated the English magnates, including Simon de Montfort. Aymer was also shown great favour, being elevated to the see of Winchester in November 1250; as arrogant and rapacious as the rest of the brood, he was both unsuitable and unpopular, and his rise added considerable fuel to the fires of resentment.

Whilst Sir Charles Oman is scath.ng on Henry's military capabilities, the king had little experience in war; he was far more inclined toward peace, an inclination that should perhaps elicit praise rather than opprobrium. One encounter wherein his generalship was required and found wanting was the combat at Taillebourg, where a strategically sited bridge over the Charente river was contested between forces led by Louis IX, his brother the Count of Poitiers, and an Anglo-French corps under Henry III and Hugh X of Lusignan. The latter had acquired the habits of a free prince; his lands were situated in the heart of Aquitaine. Poitou, under the terms of a treaty of 1214, had become a fief of the French crown. Alphonse of Poitiers was the younger brother of Louis and did not come into his own till 1240. Having reached the age of 18 he accepted the fealty of local magnates, including Hugh X, who held several valuable estates; this notion of fealty did not sit well with these powerful Poitevin barons, and they banded together to resist the count's authority; at Christmas 1241 Hugh threw down the gage (he was of course married to Isabella of Angouleme, mother of Henry III).

Matters swiftly reached a head. Louis resolved to assist his brother, and the acquiescent Poitevin lords were summoned to a muster at Chinon for Easter. With a great power the royal brothers set about reducing Hugh's bastions, whilst Henry responded by landing a force at Royan in mid-May. The king was supported by Hugh, the embittered Raymond of Toulouse and Richard of Cornwall. By the middle of June the rival forces confronted each other across the broad, lethargic sweep of the Charente, with Louis holding the Chateau de Taillebourg on the northern side, though a trial of arms was delayed until 21 July.

Henry commanded a force which Oman assesses as comprising some 1,600 knights and men-at-arms, together with 700 crossbows and an undisclosed number of foot. The bulk of all of these were raised locally; less than four-score English knights took the field that day. The French were strongly posted on the far bank with superior forces. Their only means of attacking, however, was over the bridge, where the king had established a strong block. Louis proved resourceful, having assembled a flotilla of barges; these he crammed with chosen men, supported by crossbows and prepared for an amphibious assault, whilst the remainder launched a determined assault on the bridge itself. Disheartened, the defenders gave ground, allowing the attackers to gain a lodgement on both bridge and river bank. Finding himself thus outmatched, Henry simply withdrew his forces, albeit in good order, and fought no more, dispatching Richard of Cornwall next day to seek terms. It was not a catastrophe, such as Louis himself was later to experience against the Mamelukes, but the Anglo-Lusignans abandoned their baggage and thus clearly lost the field. It was certainly far from glorious, and indicated Henry possessed no discernible flair for tactics. One cannot imagine Longshanks behaving likewise.

Simon de Montfort, sixth Earl of Leicester

Simon de Montfort is regarded as a pivotal figure in the history of the period, and indeed in the development of medieval English polity, and rightly so. Nonetheless he remains something of an enigma, possessed of high physical and moral courage, austere and unbending, harsh, censorious and frequently perceived as being largely motivated by self-interest. In part his notorious avarice was forced upon him by a continuing shortage of funds and the need to provide for his four sons. He had an almost obsessive anathema against debt, as revealed in the terms of his will,[8] a characteristic which probably informed his growing rift with his brother-in-law Henry III. His lineage was impressive: a Frenchman, he was a younger son of Simon de Montfort, titular fifth earl (1160–1218). The lords of Montfort l'Amaury near Paris were of ancient though not necessarily wealthy lineage; Simon the Elder took the cross in 1199 but soon became disenchanted when his fellow crusaders succumbed to Venetian schemes and sacked the Christian city of Zara in Dalmatia.[9]

It was to be a different crusade that would guarantee the elder Simon's fame and his renown as a great general: in 1209 he was appointed to lead an expedition against the Cathar heretics in Languedoc and chastise Raymond of Toulouse. De Montfort gained a formidable reputation in the bitter and savage war that followed. He was notorious for unbending severity and cruelty, and he exhibited the same austere and inflexible faith that was to characterize his son, developing links with the Dominicans, who were active in suppressing the heresy. He was killed at the siege of Toulouse. Through his mother, Amicia de Beaumont, he had inherited a claim to one half-share in the earldom on the death of his uncle in 1204. Three years later King John had sequestered the lands and revenues; in 1215 these passed into the control of the fourth Earl of Chester, a nephew of Simon's. In due course Simon's sons Amaury, the eldest, and Simon, the sixth earl, came to an accord whereby the latter ceded his rights in France in return for the former granting his rights in England.

When Simon arrived in England, a young, ambitious knight and ironically, like the despised Savoyards and Lusignans, a foreigner, he scored an early coup by marrying the king's sister Eleanor of England. This may, as the king later asserted in the course of a violent quarrel with Simon, have been the consequence of a clandestine liaison that resulted in pregnancy. Certainly the affair was concluded both in secret and in haste; Eleanor was the widow of William Marshal, second Earl of Pembroke, and had, on his death, sworn an oath of chastity. Her breaking of the oath subsequently caused her pious second husband much anxiety. Nonetheless she bore him seven children, including four surviving sons – Henry (named after the king), Simon the Younger, Amaury and Guy. The marriage produced a backlash from the bride's other brother, Richard of Cornwall, who went so far as to draw his sword in rebellion till the king, anxious to be all things to all men, bought him off with the sum of 6,000 marks.

Cordial relations with the king were soon soured by a violent quarrel provoked by Simon's indebtedness to Thomas II of Savoy, one of the queen's uncles. It was now that Henry accused the earl of seducing and ruining his sister. The pair felt it wise to accept temporary exile in France, but Simon was never to escape financial difficulties and the matter of Eleanor's dower from her dead husband's estate would be a running sore in his often tense relationship with the king. In 1240 he took the cross, and later served in Henry's abortive campaign of 1242 in Poitou. It would appear that Simon arrived in England with a formidable military reputation already acquired – some mystery attaches to this, as he had no real exploits to his name, and he may simply have been enjoying the benefit of association with his father's achievement. The fiasco of the French campaign left him with a jaundiced view of his brother-in-law's capabilities.

By 1248 Simon was again proposing to take the cross but accepted the offer of the governorship of unruly Gascony. His rule was both effective and harsh, exciting a string of complaints, and though he was acquitted of any wrongdoing, the king proved obdurate over monies owed and de Montfort retired in disgust to France. Influenced by his mentors Grosseteste and Adam Marsh, he made peace with Henry the following year and gave assistance when the king intervened personally in Gascony, finding out just how difficult his tumultuous subjects were and emptying his treasury in the process. The king's difficulties were exacerbated by his attempts to secure the throne of Sicily for his younger son, Edmund. Opposition from a core of magnates was becoming increasingly vocal, as the preference given to 'foreigners', the Savoyards and Lusignans, failure in Poitou, the sore of Gascony and folly of Sicily, combined with the king's despotic tendencies, undermined the validity of his rule.

The Leopard

Prince Edward, who, from his father's death in 1272, was to rule for thirty-five years, is regarded as one of England's greatest medieval sovereigns, known popularly as 'Longshanks' because of his height and impressive build,[10] 'Edward the Lawgiver', 'The English Justinian' and, most emotively, 'Hammer of the Scots'.[11] In his youth some of his contemporaries, including the chronicler Matthew Paris, regarded him as both wild and vicious,[12] and he was noted for both his hot temper and propensity for violence. The prince was named after Edward the Confessor, to whose cult, as previously noted, his father had formed a particular attachment. In November 1254 he married the 13-year-old Eleanor of Castile,[13] and in 1249 he was granted Gascony, though this was subject to de Montfort's prior appointment which, nominally at least, was for a term of seven years.

Father and son certainly quarrelled, and Matthew Paris recorded a violent row over Gascony where Edward's approach differed from his father's, and the strong-minded heir was soon entering into agreements with various Gascon factions without the king's sanction. Though he also had estates in Wales and Ireland the prince fretted under his father's controls. In political terms Edward was initially more closely identified with the Savoyard faction of his mother's relatives. Peter of Savoy had gained the honour of Richmond in 1240, and next year his brother Boniface was elevated to the archbishopric of Canterbury;[14] the prince's marriage contract was negotiated by Peter d'Aigueblanche, another Savoyard and bishop of Hereford.[15] By 1248, however, Edward seems more aligned with his Poitevin half-uncles, the hated Lusignans.

Edward's lands in Wales also proved problematic in that the prince's apparently arbitrary rule and imposition of English customs angered native Welshmen and provided fuel for the swelling ambitions of Llywelwyn. In 1256 rebellion broke out and soon assumed serious proportions, with Llywelwyn attacking not only Edward's holdings but those of the great marcher lords Mortimer and de Clare. In the following year Edward's small forces were seriously worsted in an action in the Towy Valley, and, faced by a deepening crisis, Henry abandoned his earlier policy of delegation by assuming overall personal control. As was usually the case with the king's campaigns, the affair was badly organized and botched, creating further strain on over-taxed resources with very little to show for the expenditure.

The Provisions of Oxford and the slide into war, 1258–1264

By the late 1250s Henry's government was in crisis. This had a number of causes: a disastrous foreign policy, the mire of Gascony and the idiocy of the Sicilian venture, the excesses of the Lusignans and an incompetent fiscal policy which could not begin to support the burden of the king's schemes, exacerbated by the frequent refusal of Parliament to underwrite perceived extravagances with the taxpayers' cash. Prominent amongst the magnatial opposition were men such as Gilbert de Clare, Earl of Gloucester, John fitz Geoffrey[16] and even Peter of Savoy. One notable reformer was Simon de Montfort: to civic weal was added private grudge. Simon and the king had never been fully reconciled after the business in Gascony: Simon had long held concerns over Eleanor's dower, and Henry had obligations to de Montfort arising from the latter's tenure which he simply could not afford to meet. The earl's intransigence over the question of debt undoubtedly poisoned what might otherwise have been a purely fiscal dispute. At the hearing in 1252 to investigate the complaints brought by aggrieved Gascons, Simon had received significant support from the magnates, even including the king's brother, Richard of Cornwall.

This storm, so long in brewing, erupted in 1258 when the reformers, with substantive magnatial support, including the earl of Norfolk, effectively rebelled. This was a bloodless coup which saw the detested Lusignans expelled and the royal prerogative effectively confiscated by a council of fifteen magnates. That the hated foreigners should be driven out by one who was himself a foreigner lends the situation a fine irony. It was partly Simon's military credentials which made him so attractive to his fellow reformers; should a showdown occur and swords be drawn, his experience would be most advantageous. This form of committee rule was the very antithesis of the autocratic government which the king preferred and, of course, harked back to Magna Carta. *The Song of Lewes*[17] sums up the prevailing sentiment precisely when it refers to the king's duty to rule in accordance with the public weal and, should he fail to do so, obligation of the magnates to act on behalf of both gentry and commons to correct abuses. For two years then the king ruled only by the consent of this cabal of magnates; that the king was able to once again exert full authority after 1261 was due in part to papal meddling and the powerful support of Richard of Cornwall, who had returned from his German adventure. Henry also received succour from the pope, who issued a bull absolving him of his oath. One who refused to accept the king's restored status was his brother-in-law, Simon de Montfort, who decamped to France in disgust.

An uneasy calm prevailed till 1263 when matters again began to unravel; both king and prince quarrelled with a number of magnates. The Provisions of Oxford, as laid down by the reformers in 1258, backed by binding oaths,[18] had provided for a much-needed reform of local government and the administration of justice in the shires; this was not only long overdue but played to the clamour of the gentry, a major source of support for the reformers whose affinity amongst the higher nobility was less assured. When Simon returned in 1263 it was with the intention of imposing the Provisions of Oxford upon the king and his heir. Simon was now emerging as the clear leader of the baronial faction backing reform, but this was now a more slender affinity than in 1258.

Now Simon's support was derived from his own sons, Henry, Simon the Younger, and Guy, together with magnates such as Peter de Montfort, Hugh Despenser and Walter de Cantilupe, Bishop of Worcester, inheritor of the mantle of Grosseteste. Others, a predominantly younger group, were also swayed toward the reformers' path: Nicholas of Seagrave,[19] Henry of Hastings,[20] Geoffrey de Lucy, John de Burgh, John fitz John and, above all, Gilbert de Clare, Earl of Gloucester. The citizens of London were also vociferous in their support. The urban bourgeoisie had a loud voice in the capital and, on 13 July 1263, the rowdier elements assaulted the queen as her barge was on the Thames, to the extent that the mayor, Thomas fitz Thomas, intervened to save Eleanor from injury and till she was afforded temporary refuge by the Bishop of London.

Despite having the support of the leading thinkers in the English church who were anxious for the reform of ecclesiastical abuses, in 1263 the reformers had fragile magnatial support; opprobrium did not attach to the king's personal rule. All of these men had sworn an oath to the king, and there was a reluctance to impose a brake upon his authority when many felt the lessons of 1258 had been learnt and the administration improved accordingly. As Dr Carpenter points out, many barons had personal concerns over the conduct of Simon himself. His steely resolve and adherence to the oath of 1258 might be laudable, but the substantial leavening of personal ambition and outright avarice was less edifying. In consequence, de Montfort's flaws prevented him from promoting a repeat of 1258; his influence over the magnates was insufficient to create anything more than stalemate and this was dangerous, bringing the realm to the precipice of civil war – a repeat of 1215 which most magnates were understandably anxious to avoid at all costs.

As a solution it was proposed to refer the whole matter of the king's rule and the efficacy of the Provisions of Oxford to the arbitration of Louis IX of France.[21] When the French king delivered his verdict in January 1264 he found entirely, and not unexpectedly, in favour of Henry III; the Provisions of Oxford were dismissed and the king left free to appoint whomsoever he wished as ministers, either native or foreign. For the reformers this was a serious blow: everything they had achieved since 1258 was cast down, a humiliation too far for Simon and his affinity. Far from resolving the outstanding matters between king and barons, Louis's decision pushed the realm further down the path to civil war. Realizing that hostilities were now inevitable and that London was inextricably linked to the reform faction, the king moved his court to Oxford, as Charles I would do over four centuries later. On Thursday, 3 April 1264, the royal standard was unfurled within the city – war had just been declared.

Chapter 3

Lewes (1) – The Campaign

*Lewes and Evesham show a distinct advance in the art of war,
which we may fairly set down to the influence of Simon de Montfort.*
                                              Sir Charles Oman

In his assessment of the military capabilities of King Henry
III, the great historian, as we have noted, tends to the
dismissive; he has little time for Henry, whose traditional bad
press has dogged chroniclers of the campaign of 1264. This
pejorative approach may be unjustified as the honours in the
competing strategies prior to the battle on 14 May are in fact quite
evenly distributed. When the king raised his standard at Oxford
he was well placed to deal a significant blow or series of blows
against the Montfortians. Simon's chief strengths lay firstly in the
south, where he held both London and the critical bastion of
Dover, and secondly in the Midlands, centred on his great redoubt
at Kenilworth. A score of miles and more to the north-east of this
fortress lay Leicester, the earl's borough, and, like a veritable
shield wall, the lands of his affinity clustered about – Peter de
Montfort, Hugh Despenser, Nicholas of Seagrave, Henry of
Hastings, Ralph Bassett of Drayton, Thomas of Astley, William of
Birmingham, Richard Trussel, Robert fitz Nicholas and Robert of
Hartshill. To secure the southern and eastward flank de Montfort
had garrisoned the other key bastions of Northampton[1] and
Nottingham.

Beginning the campaign: royalist moves

Enjoying the benefit of interior lines, and having driven a wedge between the twin centres of baronial affinity, the king could now move against either. Prince Edward had seen off an attempt against Gloucester, and the royalists were able to concentrate their attention on Simon's Midlands strongholds. Having failed to secure Gloucester, Simon the Younger and Peter de Montfort scurried back into Northampton, whilst Henry de Montfort and John Giffard of Brimpstead made for Kenilworth. Simon the Elder had come as far as Brackley, a day's march to the north of the king's base at Oxford; this was in March and the earl was fully appreciative of the difficulties he now faced. Consequently, he instructed the bishops of Worcester, London, Winchester and Chichester to argue the barons' case. The terms were intended to be attractive: de Montfort and his faction would now accept the decision of Louis's arbitration, a major concession subject only to the stipulation that the king would remove all foreigners from his service and appoint only English advisers. Though this was a significant and oft-repeated demand, the original Provisions of Oxford had been substantially diluted. Henry's confidence was such that he felt no compulsion to compromise.

It cannot be seen as coincidental that these peace-feelers happened to arise at the same point as fresh and violent anti-royalist disturbances in London. Richard of Cornwall's estate at Isleworth was despoiled and other known royalists suffered similar attacks on property, whilst numerous royal appointees were flung into gaol, apparently by the mob. As Dr Maddicott points out, the role of de Montfort's ally Hugh Despenser, castellan of the Tower and instigator of the sacking of Isleworth, tends rather to point the finger of suspicion in the earl's direction. Had this tactic succeeded and the king headed for his capital then the strategic advantage his position at Oxford offered would have been sacrificed – Henry was not that impetuous or naïve. When the talks foundered, de Montfort returned to London. The king's army now moved swiftly: John de Warenne and Roger of Leybourne were detached to seize Rochester and Reigate, and by 3 April the bulk of the royal army was marching on Northampton.

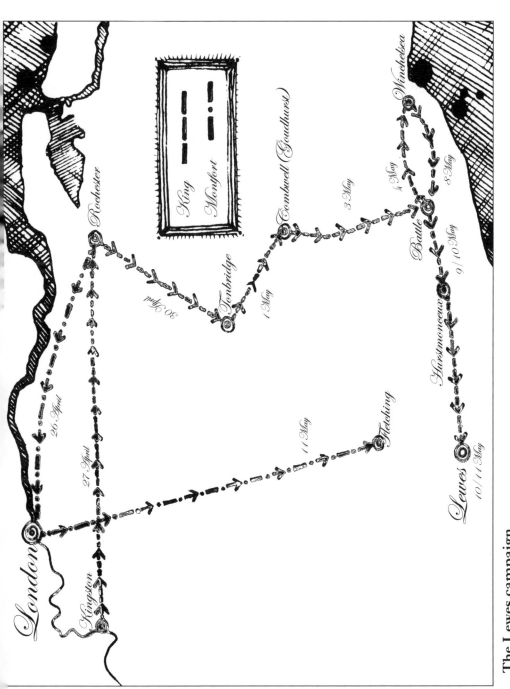

The Lewes campaign

On the 5th, facilitated by the compliance of the monks of St Andrew's Priory, the town was taken by a *coup de main*; the castle capitulated next day and a useful haul of prisoners was taken, including Simon the Younger, Peter de Montfort, Ralph Bisset, Baldwin Wake, Adam of Newmarket and some fifteen other leading knights.

For the Montfortians this was a most unfortunate beginning; worse was to follow. Leicester fell, virtually without a blow being struck, on 11 April, and Nottingham was cowed into surrender immediately after; Prince Edward seized Tutbury Castle and 'took up' the estates of the rebel Earl of Derby, Robert de Ferrers. Simon had marched from London as soon as Northampton was threatened, but its swift collapse saw him no further north than St Albans – here there was more bad news: rumours of disturbances in the capital, orchestrated by a Jewish fifth column, necessitated his immediate return. The earl spent the second week of April wielding the stick, and despoiling the Jewish community. This was done in the most brutal manner, with many being simply killed as a corollary to robbery. Given that the earl was in need of cash, theft was probably as prominent a motive as religious bigotry. One of his affinity, John fitz John, was said to have murdered a rich Jewish financier, Cok, son of Abraham, a crime he perpetrated with his bare hands; this earned no rebuke but he was obliged to part with a share of the ill-gotten gains.

Thus far, in strategic terms, the honours accrued almost entirely to the royalists. Kenilworth had not fallen and its great walls appeared inexpugnable; Henry de Montfort and Giffard had successfully sallied and taken Warwick castle but, with this notable exception, the principal baronial centres in the Midlands had been dealt with. There was now the matter of London.

The road lay open. Simon the Elder was completely wrong-footed, with bastions lost and his affinity reduced, and whilst the earl was venting his frustration in an outburst of anti-Semitism,[2] the king could consider his next move. Clearly the direction had to be southwards; there was nothing to be gained by sitting down before Kenilworth's massive ramparts. The prize had to be London and its approaches – to what extent royalist strategy thus far had been directed by the king or by the counsels of his eldest son and brother we cannot perceive. Henry was not by nature a martial ruler, but Prince Edward very clearly was, and his strategic genius was to manifest itself most pronouncedly during the Evesham campaign of the following year. To restore their doubtless flagging morale, the Montfortians required a bold stroke. Simon, whatever his other failings, was never faint-hearted; the obvious target had to be Rochester, that great, gaunt stone donjon which had defied King John near half a century before. Rochester guarded the south-eastern approaches to London; if the royalists were to blockade the city then possession was pivotal.

Rochester besieged

For Simon, moving against Rochester might also restore the strategic initiative. The king could not ignore this peril – he would have to march south, into the baronial heartland, to lift the siege. Oman is highly critical of the king for not making a dash for London after the fall of Northampton: his followers were numerous and flushed with their victory. However, this is perhaps unfair: to advance southwards with potentially hostile forces able to concentrate behind was highly risky, and politically no king wants to batter a way into his own capital – he should be seen to enter in triumph rather than storming as the oppressor. Having eliminated the threat from the Midlands there was a strong argument for simply penning the barons up in London and forcing them to negotiate from a position of weakness. To commit to battle was not the first instinct of the medieval commander: to seize the enemy's strongholds, ravage his lands and deal harshly with his people were less hazardous means of bringing an opponent to his knees. Besides, though this was civil war, there had not yet been any great effusion of blood: the knights taken at Northampton had not been mistreated or sentenced, and both sides were still in at the stage of manoeuvre, of armed diplomacy. Blood, once shed, was never easily washed away; a feud begun at Evesham between Despenser and Mortimer would still be festering in the reign of Edward II.[3]

By 17 April 1264 Rochester's leaguer was under way. Gilbert de Clare came from the south, his base being at Tonbridge, whilst de Montfort, out of London, occupied Strood on the banks of the Medway, facing the great fortress. The locals proved resolutely and energetically royalist in sentiment. The bridge was slighted, though there was sufficient remnant to form a kind of barbican jutting into the Medway. A number of probing attacks were seen off but the earl sent fireships on the evening of the 18th: the flaming vessels, sure harbinger of panic if well-handled, did their work and, in the confusion, the attackers' commanded party got into the town and next day broke into the castle; the bailey was soon theirs but not the great keep which, as before, maintained its defiance.

Henry reacted with vigour, bringing his forces south by a series of forced marches; the army, in that first full month of spring, advanced perhaps a score of miles per day. By 20 April the royalists were at Grantham, and less than a week later Henry was at Aylesbury. By dusk on the 26th his vanguard, presumably mounted, had pressed on another 45 miles into Croydon, putting them within a further day's ride of beleaguered Rochester, whose stout walls were still resisting the earl's engines. Though, as Dr Carpenter points out, this rate of advance is less spectacular than the chroniclers are inclined to suggest,[4] it remains an impressive indication of the army's logistical efficiency. We should be mindful that to move a large body of men and animals over distances on medieval roads was no easy task. The numbers involved are difficult to assess as the chronicles tend to sow confusion; these will be discussed more fully in Chapter 4, but for present purposes I intend to follow Dr Carpenter when he gives the royalists some 1,500 horse and several thousand foot. On the march these would be strung out over a dozen miles or more, with cavalry in the van and possibly bringing up the rear with the infantry marching in a long, unwieldy column, and behind them the great toiling mass of wives and followers, tradesmen, suppliers, baggage, beasts and livestock.

Such a sure riposte posed fresh problems for the Montfortians: the leaguer had drawn the royalists south but they could now choose to shift their axis of advance toward London, leaving the earl impotent before the unbreached walls, and there appear to have been continuing rumblings of mutiny in the city itself. The baronial army had to decide upon a course of action. By the 26th scouts would have given the alert that the royal van lay barely 25 miles distant, poised to strike. For de Montfort there was no viable alternative but to break up the siege and return to London: he could not afford to risk losing the city; failure before Rochester, whilst unfortunate, was less dire. On the 26th the earl's forces tramped back through the gates of the capital.[5] It is hard to assess who had gained or regained the strategic initiative, but the honours must, upon consideration, surely lie with the king. He had emasculated the opposition in the Midlands and had reacted decisively over the threat to Rochester. Simon had succeeded in drawing the royalists more toward ground of his choosing but he had failed before the walls of Rochester; Henry was free to tighten the vice around London.

Lewes: the opening moves
In the event this putative siege was not pursued with any noticeable vigour. Prince Edward with a commanded body of horse reconnoitred the city's defences but nothing more was attempted. Again Oman and, following on, Colonel Burne, see this as grounds for censure. It must, however, be borne in mind that the royal army would have been quite exhausted by their fatiguing marches and not necessarily in any proper state to carry out major offensive operations. Instead there was mopping up: on 27 April the royalists back-tracked to deal with de Clare's hold at Kingston before pushing on to Rochester and driving off the token force de Montfort had left to maintain the pretence of leaguer. The king was at the castle by 28 April and those of the baronial affinity who fell into his hands were dealt with severely.[6]

De Clare's castle at Tonbridge was the next to fall, its colours struck on 30 April. At this point the royalist strategy seems to unravel, earning strong criticism from Oman and Burne. The Battle Abbey Chronicle asserts that securing the adherence of the Cinque Ports was the immediate priority.[7] If so, this is difficult to fathom: perhaps the royalists, buoyed by their successes and confident in their number, thought de Montfort already beaten and that mopping-up operations were thus the only tactical requirements. This seems unlikely: Henry and his loyal magnates knew the calibre of man who opposed them, and no amount of hubris could have blinded them to the reality that Simon de Montfort was very far from being defeated. True, the campaign had gone very badly for him – repulsed at Gloucester, beaten at Northampton, robbed of Leicester and Nottingham, twice sent scurrying back to London and frustrated at Rochester. Perhaps the royalists also had hopes of their supporters within the capital who might yet be able to open the gates without a fight.

Nonetheless, on 6 May de Montfort once again marched his army out. His one strategic gain had been to draw his enemies south and now south-east – this was his sole advantage, and he could not afford to shirk the challenge. His hand was greatly strengthened by the royalists, who, having abandoned their central axis, had permitted the rump of his survivors in the Midlands to come up from Kenilworth. Henry de Montfort and John Giffard marched to London; Derby failed to appear, as was no doubt the case with many others, but at least the earl now had, if not substantial forces, then sufficient for the task at hand. The royalists had given the earl a respite; from now on it was he who would dictate the strategy of the campaign and he who would initiate the decisive encounter. As Carpenter points out, this was a defining moment: by putting his army on the road to confrontation de Montfort was committing it to battle, an encounter that was bound to decide the campaign; for the barons, if they failed, their lands and lives, the futures of their lines, were all at hazard. It was a courageous decision.

For the royalists their 'March to the Sea' through the undulating and heavily forested byways of the Weald was by no means easy. The Weald of Kent and Sussex, the trees now with their fresh green cloak of spring, was bad ground for a large conventional force; its ways were narrow and confusing, and the great mass of wildwood had the effect of a smothering shroud. As the threads of mounted men-at-arms, columns of straggling foot and the great unwieldy tail stumbled uncertain through a veritable maze of tracks, they were constantly in fear of unseen attackers, either local outlaws and opportunists or commanded parties of Montfortians left behind as guerrillas. It was unsafe for a knight to move without the reassuring carapace of harness. One who was not so well protected was the royal chef who on 2 May, whilst passing the priory of Comberwell, Goudhurst in Kent, was sniped by an archer. Henry III was notoriously fond of his creature comforts and, finding his personal staff so denuded, took fearful revenge and ordered the execution of 315 prisoners who, possibly having been rash enough to come forward under the aegis of a proposed amnesty, were parted from their heads that very evening:

> beheaded in the Weald in the parish of St. Mary, Ticehurst, in the place called Flimwell in the presence of the king, all of whom had been called deceitfully to the king's peace only then to occur that death through the counsel of Richard, king of Germany.[8]

Next to incur royal displeasure was the abbot of Battle Abbey, who was summarily fined 100 marks on account of the fact that some of those who had lost their heads at Flimwell had been his tenants.

Freed from the dangerous confines of the forest, the royalists reached Winchelsea by the end of the first week in May. Here they eased their former tensions with liberal imbibing, and Henry received the customary assurances from the burgesses of the Cinque Ports – their ships would be needed for any blockade of London. We may discern here some sensible strategic thinking: the blockade of London was no small affair, and to be effective the king would need a fleet to control the Thames; without access to adequate numbers of vessels, the operation could not proceed further with any prospect of success.

No one in the royal army appears to have foreseen the bold move which de Montfort had initiated. By 9 May the king had returned to Battle; his immediate plan was to attend a muster in Canterbury in three days' time and then take a view as to whether to eliminate the Montfortians holding Dover or to leave these unmolested in rear and turn his attention toward London.

Rather than go to Canterbury he summoned the Kentish contingent to join him, then led the army from Battle to Lewes, a score of miles west. One night, either the 9th or 10th, was spent bivouacked at Hurstmonceaux, where a rich bag of game, hunted through the park, provided fresh meat. With his scouts probing for news and sightings of the baronial army, the royalists moved with care, fully harnessed and prepared for a sudden deployment, should the need arise.[9]

Lewes, as most commentators agree was, in the circumstances, a sound choice. The town was walled and protected by a strong castle, and the castellan, John de Warenne, Earl of Surrey, was a staunch partisan who had already done exemplary service by holding Rochester. From the king's personal perspective the agreeable Cluniac priory of St Pancras, which lay just beyond the circuit of walls at Sandover, provided a most comfortable billet;[10] Prince Edward appears to have preferred the more austere confines of the castle itself.

A Saxon township, Lewes stood below the rise of the Downs where the river Ouse slices through; to the east the land swoops down to the water so that the houses of Cliffe cling to the banks. Looking west the ground is more level, rippling with dip and swell till it begins the gentle climb to the downland above. The town in the thirteenth century was bounded to the north by the ramparts of de Warenne's castle and to the south by the priory, whose grounds extended to 20 acres and more[11] and which now played host to the King of England and his entourage. The river at this time was tidal and navigable, the alluvial ground south of the priory a morass of dank pools and shifting banks. The loop in the Ouse covered the town on the northern and eastern flanks; the marsh effectively sealed the southern approach, and to the west were the formidable walls of the fortress. For a defender this had advantages but equally presented tactical challenges. Accepting that any attack would come from the west the defender had either to be prepared to man the castle walls, fortify the priory and barricade the streets, or attempt to retire to the east bank of the Ouse. If it was his wish to fight then he must sally westwards from the town and contest the rise of the Downs beyond.

This was to prove crucial to the conduct of the battle, and it is toward the ridge above the houses that we must now direct our attention. The gradient is by no means severe as the high ground declines toward the Ouse; the slope is not, however linear – rather it is formed by three slight projections or spurs, each split by a shallow defile. The easternmost of these spurs is now traversed by the Lewes–Offenham road (the A275). With the royalists encamped at Lewes, de Montfort took station by Sheffield and Fletching (which were in his ownership), some eight miles north of the town; though these hamlets had no walls they remained surrounded by the great forest which, as Carpenter observes, would prove equally effective.[12]

Though he had come ready to offer battle, de Montfort was canny enough to perceive the wisdom of making a further, final attempt at brokering a negotiated settlement. This was eminently sensible, for not only was the baronial army outnumbered but no magnate, however secure he might be in the justice of his cause, would lightly bear arms against his sovereign: to do so would be a mortal sin, as the king was the Lord's anointed and thus inviolate; to attack his person directly struck at the very core of the feudal pyramid and was thus anathema. To a man of de Montfort's strong religious convictions this was a matter of the very gravest weight. For current purposes I propose to concur with Carpenter and suggest negotiations were entered into on 12 May.[13] The earl sent a delegation comprising the Bishop of Chichester[14] and several Dominican and Franciscan friars: the essence of the barons' proposal was a reversion to the terms of the Provisions of Oxford, subject to arbitration by suitably qualified lay and clerical experts and, crucially, a substantive offer of cash compensation to the amount of £30,000, a very considerable sum. The requirement to dismiss foreign advisers and so on remained.

Henry as *Rex Pacificus* may have been minded to consider these terms, but his brother and son counselled against; neither would countenance even such moderate fetters on the exercise of the royal prerogative. Even a watered-down version of the Provisions of Oxford would impose a level of restriction on the authority of the crown which was unprecedented and, to a mettlesome prince, intolerable. The negotiating table was now bare, and only force of arms remained. On the 13th both sides exchanged bellicose challenges – the barons maintained they were not drawing their swords against the king but to remove 'certain persons amongst those who surround you'. The king retorted with some venom: 'We therefore value not your faith or love, and defy you as their enemies.' Richard and Prince Edward, doubtless included in the barons' list of undesirables, added their own challenge:

> We therefore let you know that you are all defied as public enemies by each and all of us your enemies, and that henceforth whenever occasion offers we will with all our might labour to damage your persons and property.[15]

Battle lines were most emphatically now drawn. Edward, according to *The Song of Lewes*, wanted to see the barons grovel in halters; Richard of Cornwall was inflamed by 'pride and thirst for revenge'.[16]

Advance to contact

On 12 May, (following Gilson and Carpenter's assessment), the Montfortians sent out a commanded body, presumably mounted, to reconnoitre the high downland west of the town. Royal scouts were alert and a squadron was dispatched to observe the observers. This was a business of outposts: neither side was particularly looking to bring on a general engagement. The royalists, in ascending the ridge, espied their enemy 'in the valleys near a wood'. I concur with Carpenter, who fixes the royalists atop Mount Harry, which dips sharply to the north into a belt of fine arable soil, girded to the north by a belt of heavier clay; in the mid-thirteenth century this ground was heavily wooded. De Montfort's forces were deployed or marshalled on the better land in front of the belt of trees.[17] Both sides were content to stand their individual ground and offer no further provocation; de Warenne broke a few spears with some of Simon's scouts or perhaps foragers who probably scrimmaged in the area of Coombe Hollow. Nothing was decided; the outpost bickering flared and died before the royalists, around midday, withdrew into Lewes.

With all hopes of a peaceful outcome extinguished Simon, the following day, moved his entire power marching eastwards, skirting the rim of the downs and probably taking up a line between the villages of Offham and Hamsey.[18] With letters of defiance exchanged, the barons symbolically withdrew their fealty and committed themselves to battle; indeed it appears likely that de Montfort was hoping his manoeuvre would provoke a response and draw the royalists out to fight – given the disparity of odds the royalists were showing a surprising lack of enthusiasm for battle. This reluctance speaks more of the king than of his son and brother, both of whom were clearly anxious to try conclusions. But if Simon hoped to fight on the 13th he was disappointed, and he therefore determined to bring on a contest the next day; he had the tactical initiative and he was determined not to relinquish it.

Tactics would, as ever, be dictated by the ground; to the east of Lewes the line of the River Ouse curtailed any attack, and the ground on the west bank, whilst it offered an approach to the town from the north, was wet and hemmed in by rising ground, a funnel in which an attacker could be caught and held. It may be that Simon's objective, in drawing up his forces on the 13th, was to provoke the royalists into advancing from the south into this arena, but they wisely declined the challenge. This offered only one practical approach – from the west and the summit of the Downs. Control of this high ridge was thus of the essence, equally so to both sides, and to seize the ground de Montfort committed his army to a night march. Carpenter here parts company with both Oman and Burne, who favour an early morning advance from Fletching (an assumption drawn from interpretation of the *Chronicle of William de Rishanger*). These authorities also favour an ascent to the summit of the ridge via the track leading south-westwards from Offham, but the Gilson fragment clearly states the baronial army 'came to Boxholte' – this has been identified as a location some 500 yards south-west of Blackcap, three miles north-west of the town of Lewes and a good mile and three-quarters west of Offham.[19]

It was, as Carpenter believes, via an ancient way that leads uphill from Blackcap that the baronial army ascended to the higher ground. Simon had stolen a march on the king's army and placed himself in a strong tactical position. Some sentries had been posted but these proved unpardonably negligent. A small party had been posted there on the 13th but, lacking any relief, most had simply slipped back into Lewes, leaving only one man to keep vigil. This unfortunate individual had drifted comfortably into sleep beneath a handy gorse bush – he became the barons' first prisoner.[20] From Boxholte the army could march along the rim of the ridge; presumably, at this point, the brigades were marshalled into columns ready to deploy into line, and battle was now inevitable.[21] Their advance brought them to a level plateau upon which the south-eastern flank of the racecourse now lies.[22]

Here, as dawn was breaking on the 14th around five, the massed ranks and files looked down on a broad panorama, lit by the spring sunrise: Lewes, the town dominated by the rearing castle keep and high bell-tower of the priory, was spread before them; most importantly the ground was bare of their enemies. Here on the ridge of the South Downs in the first wash of light de Montfort knighted, as was customary, a number of his followers, including Gilbert de Clare. The earl also treated his soldiers to a rousing address – their cause, he assured them, was just; they fought for God and for England. All now knelt to seek the Lord's blessing and made confession as the chaplains moved amongst them; medieval men would not willingly set out upon their deaths, their souls still heavy burdened with sin. White crosses were pinned or hastily sewn onto surcoats, intended both to distinguish friend from foe and to solicit the Almighty's favour. Rishanger tells us that it was Walter de Cantilupe, Bishop of Worcester, who officiated, though the chronicler asserts the due observances were made before the army marched. In such circumstances and at such a moment when his life, lands and treasure are at risk a man needs all the spiritual sustenance he can muster; these men knew that the idyllic scene before them was, very soon, to be utterly transformed into something rather different. The Battle of Lewes was about to begin.

Chapter 4

Lewes (2) – The Battle

*A most signal exhibition of foresight and skill on the one side,
and of presumption and rashness on the other.*

Sir James Ramsay

Simon de Montfort's men knew their stations; they had sought God's forbearance and were ready for the hazard of battle. The baronial right flank was given to de Montfort's sons, Harry, Simon and Guy, with both John de Burgh and Humphrey Bohun; their brigade stood on a straight north–south axis reaching as far as Houndean Bottom. The centre, under de Clare, John fitz John and William de Munchensay, took station on the ridge, behind ground now occupied by the present reservoir. The right, made up mainly of Londoners, was commanded by the pairing of Nicholas of Seagrave with Henry of Hastings, supported by John Giffard and Hervey of Borham. These townsmen were almost certainly formed as a solid phalanx of foot with a thin line of horsemen to the front; before they began their advance downhill they probably stood on ground now covered by modern development west of the present Nevil Road. Generally the cavalry would be placed before the infantry whilst Simon himself held his own brigade in reserve, assisted by the London constable, Thomas of Pulesdon. Though the barons had dealt with the negligent sentries, so mighty an array could not long go unnoticed atop the Downs. As light filtered through and the spring sun began to rise, the alarum, most likely brought by pages

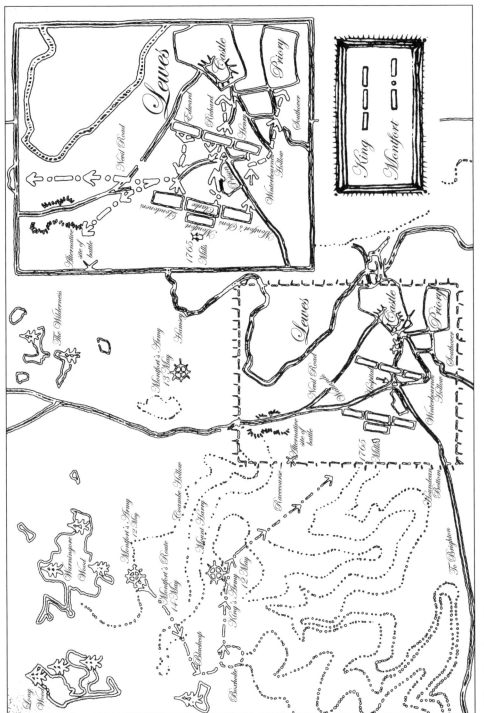

The Battle of Lewes

foraging for fodder to feed the destriers, was raised in Lewes – 'Tubis terribiliter clangentibus',[1] a most emotive description – harsh braying of war-trumpets offending the morning calm. Rishanger insists that Simon's scouts had beaten up the foragers and killed at least a couple.

Deployments

For the royalists this was indeed, in the modern idiom, 'a wake-up call'; the entire strategic position had been reversed and Simon, with a potent mix of luck, daring, resolution and skill, had brought about a fight on his own terms; the royalists' strategic gains all stood to be undone. Now the king's army spilled from the streets and confines, from castle and priory, the morning calm savagely rent by the red-faced cursing of sergeants as they struggled to set horse and foot in order – men into their companies, these into brigades. In its favour, the army had marched as a cohesive force since the commencement of the campaign and the men would know their places; there would have been a riot of confusion and of colour – fine silk banners and gorgeous trappers of the knights – as the host swelled beyond the town.

If we follow Guisborough, and most writers seem to agree upon this,[2] the royalists deployed in three brigades. Prince Edward, de Warenne, and the prince's half-uncles Guy de Lusignan and William de Valence took station on the right. Richard of Cornwall and his son Henry led the centre, bolstered by three of Scotland's greatest magnates, Robert de Bruce, John Baliol and John Comyn. Cornwall's numbers were swollen by troops of lightly armed Scottish spears and the retinues of John fitz Alan and Henry Percy. The king led the left in person, and with him stood the Earl of Hereford, (whose heir fought under de Montfort's banner, so keen was the division).

The Battle Chronicle agrees that Prince Edward was encamped in and around the castle, forming up by the Paddock and Wallands.[3] Cornwall was posted by the priory and what was then Antioch Street, using what is now High Street to muster fully west of St Anne's church whilst King Henry, coming via

Southover High Street, deployed his brigade on the Hides.[4] De Montfort had two key tactical advantages: first, he had chosen his ground and was well placed to launch a downhill assault which would, to some degree, offset his relative paucity of numbers, and, second, despite being outnumbered, he had retained a flexible tactical reserve under his own hand, whilst the royalists had none. Nonetheless the king advanced with great resolution, insists Rishanger, his royal standard 'portending the judgement of death, which they call the "Dragon"'.

This brings us to the thorny question of numbers. Carpenter considers the levy of foot which Longshanks is recorded as having mustered for his later campaigns: the infantry who served in Wales were significantly inferior in numbers to those who later campaigned in Scotland, ranging from 3,000–4,000 in the first instance to four times that number in the latter. Evidence of casualties extracted from the primary sources, supported by the later discovery of grave pits (see Appendix 2), may help, but is far from conclusive. We know the royal army, notwithstanding normal wastage and troops detached for garrison duty at Tonbridge, still enjoyed a discernible superiority; in terms of cavalry this might have been as high as three to one – 1,500 as opposed to 500.[5] We could perhaps assume, and this is largely conjecture, that the barons deployed, say, 4,000 foot and the royalists 6,000–7,000. If these figures, for want of any better, may be agreed upon, then what is not agreed upon is the course of the action. Burne is convinced the fight began with a charge delivered by Prince Edward against the Londoners on de Montfort's left who remained supine, whilst Carpenter favours an advance to contact by both sides.

Colonel Burne, an experienced soldier whose views must command our respect (and he is supported by Ramsay), points out that it was probably the prince's division that was the first to be alerted and the first royalist formation to deploy, and that the brigade mainly comprised mounted troops who could cover the distance of some three-quarters of a mile to the top of the ridge, allowing for mustering, in under ten minutes. Edward was aggressive and spurred by the impetuosity of youth. Burne also points out the considerable animosity the headstrong prince felt toward these Londoners who had but recently abused the queen, his mother.[6] Carpenter takes an entirely different view, based upon his interpretation of the sources and an exhaustive investigation of the ground. He points out that the royalists had deployed not over level terrain but upon a field which, though level in the centre, falls away on both the northern and southern flanks, into the Paddock and Wallands in the former instance and down toward Houndean Bottom, Winterbourne Hollow and Southover in the latter. This has the crucial effect of putting the right of each army out of sight of the left of the other; de Montfort, holding his reserve in the baronial centre, atop the ridge could, by adjusting his position slightly, appreciate the full scope of events – a most singular advantage.

Blaauw, Oman and Lord Chelwood were of the view advocated most recently by Carpenter that the main clash of arms occurred somewhere on the slope rather than along the ridge-line above. The location of grave pits by the prison would tend to support this view, as there was no imperative to remove casualties any great distance from where they had fallen. The Gilson fragment is quite precise in setting the fight some way down the slope, with the baronial army advancing as far as a mill outside the Lewes leper hospice, and that contact occurred in the vicinity.[7] We may assume that the hospital was that of St Nicholas, which stood where the primary school now stands and opposite the present gaol – it was customary, for obvious reasons, for leper houses to be situated outside towns. Mention of a mill also arises in the London Chronicle (*Chronicles of the Reigns of Edward I and Edward II*), which supports Gilson, mentioning an advance to contact by both armies; the Lewes Chronicle actually gives a name to this feature, the mill *suelligi*.[8] The exact location has exercised several generations of historians, though Carpenter favours that shown on seventeenth-century maps and standing some 200 yards or so east of the hospital. This would have been a prominent landmark for any descending from the ridge, close to the then leper house.[9]

Prince Edward's charge

What is certainly agreed is that the first clash on this fine spring morning took place between the royal right under Prince Edward and de Montfort's left, led by Seagrave and Hastings with the Londoners. Nor is there any doubt as to the outcome. The prince's knights were marshalled in their squadrons by the Paddock and Wallands. These bold young paladins would have thrown on harness at the first alarum, pages cursing and fumbling with buckles and straps. Before they mounted each would have been encased in a fine mesh of mail, not light but flexible and worn by one long accustomed to it. In the already rising heat they also wore padded undergarments, proud surcoat with blazon of arms, sword and heater-shaped shield, the padded hood, mail coif, then the great helm, shutting down vision to a narrow slit, dimming the noise of preparation around. Few of these men would have fought in a full-scale melee before, but they were, for the most part, young, confident of their arms and lineage, led by a prince of heroic bearing and charisma, ready for the fight, blood already pounding and the red mist ready to fall.

Arrayed in their lines the proud destriers would be alerted by the scent of anticipation, as spirited as the knights they were to bear. When the trumpets blared the lines would move forward at the walk, the pace apparently a good deal more leisured than later film portrayals might suggest, cohesion being more important than speed. After three-quarters of a mile, mostly at a walk, the pace quickens to a slow trot, the hoof-beats extending in a steady drumming, spring dawn alive with the jangle of harness and tack; at perhaps 150 yards the squadrons gather speed to a fast trot, and at 50 yards out they are at a canter. Now the thunder of the charge drowns out senses, roars across the empty downland; the line of enemy, etched in the narrow slit, swells to fill the vision; individual pennons and then figures become distinct. Lances couched and shifted, selecting the target, marking the man, judging speed, stiffening for the shock of impact that slams the rider back against the high cantle, jars along the nerves and muscle of arm and shoulder.

Prince Edward's cavalry brigade smashed into the mounted

screen fronting the footmen from London: rout seems to have been virtually instantaneous – the baronial horse were simply swept aside. John Giffard was taken, a number were slain, and the Earl of Oxford, Geoffrey de Lucy and Humphrey de Bohun favoured discretion, though the latter did not escape without wounds.[10] Some writers, particularly Oman, have ascribed a measure of faint-heartedness to the Montfortian knights, but it is likely the odds against them were long and the matter quickly decided. This now left the foot exposed, unsupported and undoubtedly demoralized, quite likely disordered by the slew of riders and riderless horses; if they stood it was not for long, very probably stirrings of panic having already rippled through the lines. A trickle from the rear turned to a steady stream and swelled inexorably to a torrent, unstoppable as the foot stampeded up the slope down which they had just marched and scattered. The grave pits or possible burial sites identified by the chalk pits may contain the bones of those who were hacked down in the rout; some few remains found by the Wallands may represent those who fell in first contact – the relative paucity of such inhumations could suggest that casualties in the fight were few.

As later commanders, including Charles I, were to realize, it is one thing to launch a successful charge: it is quite another to exploit the success. Henry III was to discover this as his son's mounted brigade disappeared from the field like hounds scenting the fox, careering over the killing field of the open downs. Prince, barons and knights took vengeance on these fractious city-dwellers, the urban hoi polloi who had helped fracture the ordered calm of the realm. The pursuit was long, unchecked and bloody; Guisborough claims that three score gentlemen in addition to many of the commons drowned or were slain attempting to ford the Ouse.[11] As a tactical victory, Edward's was complete, but his inability to rein in and regroup deprived the king of what was in all probability the very flower of his chivalry, the prince himself, de Warenne, de Valence, Hugh Bigod, Roger Mortimer and the other marcher lords. The chroniclers agree the pursuit was extended, scattering over two to four miles, knots of mounted men swerving to pluck a ripe group of fugitives and manure the downland soil with their blood. How many of the commons were slaughtered cannot be ascertained, but this would easily run into the hundreds. It is recorded the Londoners did not slow down till the spire of St Paul's came into view.[12]

In terms of the wider course of the battle the royalist right was as effectively removed as the baronial left: the triumph of one and the rout of the other was to have no bearing on the final outcome. Burne allows some 40 minutes for the unchecked pursuit at an average speed of 6 mph; the chroniclers are vague as to exact timings but we are led to assume that the fight began shortly after first light and the initial clash occurred very soon in the day. Burne, however, suggests Edward put his attack in at around 10 am, which, if we allow an hour for the rout and pursuit, would bring us to 11 am. In this he obviously puts the start of the battle some hours beyond dawn, allowing a longer period for marshalling and manoeuvre of the hosts; he may very well be correct. Given that the process of regrouping the tired men and exhausted horses would consume several, and for the prince, tense and frustrating hours, it is unlikely the royalist right could be got back to the field much before early afternoon, say around 2 pm. By then matters on the field had already been decided, and the belated return of this powerful force could not affect the outcome.

One of the anomalies of this initial part of the fight is the presence and importance of what is described as Simon's 'chariot' – this was in fact a coach which had been especially constructed so that the earl could travel, notwithstanding a broken leg he had sustained earlier. By the time of the battle this conveyance was not strictly necessary: the troublesome injury having healed, he retained the vehicle, probably as a form of travelling HQ – one is immediately reminded of Field Marshal Montgomery's caravans. A dispute arises as to where this may have been located when the battle opened. Some suggest it was atop the ridge-line, with the earl's banner proudly displayed. This would possibly have had a morale-boosting purpose, but Burne, who dwells on the subject, remains somewhat cynical. He does not feel the army would drag such a cumbersome article on their final approach – this is sensible – and that the vehicle was left with the rest of the army's train which, according to Burne, was in the vicinity of Offham. Sir Charles Oman, however, is content to place the chariot and train quite close to the action.

If we follow Carpenter there is no reason why the baggage should have been left at Offham, this being off the line of march; Boxholte seems more likely. It is clear that, at some point, Edward's cavalry beat up the train, killing in the process several wretched Londoners cowering in the coach; these unfortunates were not rebels but hostages. Silenced by the keen-edged blades of the royalists they sprawled unheard, 'collateral damage', as such victims are now dismissed. It is not clear when the attack on the train occurred: Guisborough is adamant that the incident took place after the rally, on the royalists' return toward Lewes. Notions that Simon placed the coach to act as some form of bait seem far-fetched; he had decided, from the outset, to assume the offensive, so such ruses had no obvious place in his strategy.

Rishanger takes a different view altogether, asserting that the baggage train was taken with the army and parked on the summit of the ridge, and that the chariot was placed centrally within the leaguer and a strong guard posted. The Melrose chronicler gives a description of the carriage which, he says, was covered in iron plates. There were only two London burgesses who had been arrested as known royalist partisans: both were elderly and kept confined, the war-wagon having only a single narrow access, which had been sealed up the evening before. Furthermore, this writer insists the carriage was decked with banners to provide a lure and that this proved effective in that a part of Prince Edward's division frittered several valuable hours trying to force an entry on the assumption Simon was within. This may mostly be considered fanciful. Nonetheless, we can be sure the baggage train was not undefended; a company of chosen men under William le Blound, a fervent reformer, was detailed to protect the wagons, and they fulfilled their task most valiantly, being entirely cut down. William was one of the few gentry casualties on the baronial side.

Trial by battle

We now switch our attention to the other flank, where de Montfort's right collided with King Henry's left. Here the ground favoured the barons, the royalists very probably losing vital cohesion on the more difficult terrain around the Hides and Winterbourne Hollow. The fighting was fierce and prolonged; neither side could claim the advantage. Once contact was initiated conduct of the fight passed from the commanders to their men: this was a soldiers' battle – no careful, neatly ordered world of counters upon a map but the brutal, hard-fought frenzy of the melee. Men struggled forward, great clouds of dust and steam rising around them; humans and horses sweated prodigiously, and without water both would swiftly be reduced by dehydration. If harness was lighter than the dead-weight of myth, it was no cooler, and fighting men soon felt the furnace heat enveloping them. Thirst and heatstroke would do the job of wounds. In combat a man needed water and respite. Several accounts of battles[13] relate that, from time to time, combatants would draw apart by mutual consent to reorder their lines and assuage their raging thirsts.

In the fight a harnessed man was unlikely to be felled by the first cut; with limbs slashed and useless he would be beaten to the ground in a flurry of blows then dispatched by a dagger or bill thrust either through the eye-slit or unarmoured groin. His vision restricted, his hearing dimmed, surrounded by dust and dirt, stamping, and the slashing frenzy of the spears, the medieval fighting man faced a most unenviable struggle. If he survived uninjured he was indeed fortunate; even minor injuries could fester and kill. It was such a tableau that now spilled, relentless in its fury, across the pastoral landscape of the Downs, lines bucking and heaving, coming together then parting, shuffling in realignment, a carpet of writhing anguished humanity, dead and dying. Contemporary illustrations show a multitude of severed limbs and heads scattered over the field, and so it would be here, for the struggle was hard-fought with neither side giving ground.

Archery seems to have played only a minor role in the fight: crossbowmen were present, and at least one of the chronicle sources makes mention of slingers attached to de Montfort's army. The main contest appears to have been fought on horseback with the foot playing a secondary role. As Sir Charles Oman points out, bows are only mentioned once, during the king's difficult and tense marches through the wild forests of the Weald; the famous arrow-storm is not a feature of this battle.

At some point de Montfort committed his reserve and it was probably this which tipped the scales; his standard-bearer and Ralph Haringod fell in the melee. On the king's side so did William of Wilton, a judge; William of Axmouth, clerk and paymaster, later succumbed to his wounds. Another justiciar, Philip Basset, would not lay down his sword though he had sustained a score of gashes;[14] Fulk fitz Warin is said by Rishanger to have died by drowning. These were brave men who fought well, as did the king himself – if he failed as a statesman he did not flinch as a knight; two mounts were killed beneath him, his harness belaboured by blows. It appears that the rot began in the royalist centre, where Richard of Cornwall's brigade was first to falter. As his men recoiled, de Montfort choosing his moment to perfection flung his reserve against the king on the rebel right.

There was no rout: the fresh numbers thrown into the fight and the adverse slope conferred a very definite advantage, but the royalist left, deserted by the right and with the centre in disarray, seems to have fallen back in reasonable order. Where the modern gaol now stands the king's brigade staged a stubborn stand, giving household knights the chance to disengage and escort Henry back into the relative security of the priory; to all intents and purposes the battle proper was ended. Many on the royalist side were less fortunate, being pushed back into the uncertain and marshy plain before the river. Here the tide was up, and whilst a few swam to safety, others were sucked whole into the glistening, deadly embrace of alluvial mud. Lanercost records that, next day upon the ebb, scores of dead men and horses were exposed, the wretched, mud-soaked corpses still fixed in their saddles (Fitz Warin was most likely one of these).

Burne suggests that the king regained his sanctuary around noon, whilst his brother, the wrack of his force around, was constrained to take refuge in a windmill, most probably that identified as Snelling's mill, lying between the hospital and St Anne's church. For a time he was able to hold out whilst the place was surrounded by his enemies. His position was a most uncomfortable one: of all of the king's affinity he was perhaps the most generally reviled, and if the barons' men could not break in, he had little prospect of a successful sally. For a while the stand-off continued with a barrage of insults: 'Come out you bad miller!' the victors jeered.[15] At this point, as Burne observes, Richard might have preferred he had not written yesterday's angry letter, brimming with wrath. His position was hopeless and he was, at length, obliged to capitulate; if this was a nervous moment, his fears are understandable. Happily for him, de Montfort had no wish for a bloodbath, and 'the King of the Romans' was simply incarcerated in Kenilworth, his role in the war at an end. With him, and presumably formed with his brigade, were taken several of the Scottish gentlemen, including Robert Bruce and John Comyn; according to Rishanger, an unspecified number of knights and commons from north of the border fell.

If the issue was decided, the fighting was by no means over. The royalists had been worsted on the left and at the centre, those at the latter broken and on the former driven back. This notwithstanding, they retained significant forces in the field, and Prince Edward's powerful mounted brigade, flushed with victory and having suffered, at worst, trifling losses, might be expected to return at any time. Longshanks would be bound to renew the fight. In the meantime the carnage was spilling into the streets of Lewes town, a series of untidy scrimmages erupting as both sides jockeyed for possession. The king's men had retained their grip on the castle and any rushed attempts at an escalade were seen off without difficulty. Carpenter believes it was now no later than mid-morning, though I suspect, like Burne, it was nearer noon.

Fighting in the streets was confused, undirected and inconclusive. The king's household knights had regained the priory which was put into a defensible state; the royalist line was beaten but holding. We have no exact tally of the dead, and must rely on the chroniclers and the evidence from grave-finds.

Casualties amongst the gentry on both sides were light – no men of high rank lost their lives. The chroniclers agree that the bulk of the fallen were from the commons, anywhere between 2,000 and 2,700 in total. A good number of these would have been the wretched Londoners; more, on both sides, would have perished in the melee, with the royalists bearing the brunt. In addition to his losses in the fight, the king would have many wounded and yet more who had already fled his banners.

Both sides held their collective breath: de Montfort had taken the field but had yet to win a clear victory. The royalists had sustained major tactical reverses and were penned behind their ramparts in the castle and priory: both were formidable obstacles and could yet deny the barons an outright win. There was little to be gained in street-fighting for either commander; this would be confused, wasteful and ultimately pointless. We may consider the townspeople shivering in dread anticipation – nobody welcomes a riot of soldiery, drunk on blood and bent upon spoil. For a moment there was stalemate. Burne, as we have seen, delays the time of Prince Edward's return to around 2 pm.

The picture which greeted Edward was scarcely encouraging: his father's forces were beaten from the field, his uncle captive and the survivors penned up. Longshanks was never faint-hearted and immediately prepared to resume the fight; Simon was ready and arrayed his forces accordingly. We cannot be entirely sure where this confrontation occurred though it may have been in the centre on the rise of the saddle. We cannot indeed be certain that there was a fight at all. If the prince was ready his affinity was perhaps less enthusiastic, perceiving the king's cause in ruins; Warenne, de Valence, Hugh Bigod and Guy de Lusignan quit the field. With these defections Edward could not hope to press the attack; he had to salvage what he could, circling the town, first hailing the castle and finding the king not there, eventually taking his survivors into the priory enceinte. Henry III thus had no reserve left, and the only instrument which might have secured victory was blunted by the defection of so many magnates.

Though far from good the situation was by no means hopeless, and fighting erupted again during the afternoon. De Montfort renewed his attack on the castle, deluging the narrow streets with flaming shafts to burn out the survivors clinging to the buildings, and also attacked the priory. Lewes burned, its timber buildings in such narrow confines horribly vulnerable; the priory church also succumbed to the flames, but neither here nor in the castle did the royalists give an inch of ground – the attacks were again blunted. Prince Edward, having regrouped the forces available in the priory and with the rump of his following, including Mortimer and the Marchers, still game, prepared for a sally: 'having gathered together many of his followers, since he still retained a number of warlike men, [Edward] planned to go out again to fight'.[16]

The 'Mise' of Lewes

Though he still had the upper hand Simon's position was far from secure. He did not want to precipitate a general attack on the priory which could see the King of England and his eldest son, together with so many noble knights, killed; equally he could not risk a successful breakout – a siege risked fresh contingents of royalists coming up and another trial of arms. None of these possibilities appealed: what the earl needed was a quick solution, a negotiated peace. One expedient was the threat to put to death the royalist prisoners: these included Richard of Cornwall, the earls of Hereford and Arundel, William Bardolf, Robert de Tateshale, Roger de Somery, Henry Percy and the badly wounded Philip Basset, but Edward had taken John Giffard and his neck could be used to balance the scales. If threats could not avail then it was time for diplomacy – as the shadows lengthened into evening on the 14th and on the morning of the 15th, envoys clad in the pacific hues of the clergy shuttled back and forth. Both sides had much to debate, and the gathering of magnates at the king's table that night cannot have been a cheerful one.

Henry III, for all his failings, preferred peace to war. Even his bellicose son could detect the extreme weakness of their present position; any resumption of hostilities could only bring fresh disasters. De Montfort appeared to hold the aces, but his position remained vulnerable unless a workable accord could be brokered. The bones of the deal rested upon the Provisions of Oxford, the core of the baronial manifesto; to these the king now proposed to acquiesce. We can only imagine the reaction of his son to such surrender, but there were important concessions. The first of these concerned the Provisions themselves: though they were to stand as drafted in the first instance a further process of review and arbitration would be entered into.[17] Second, and this was to have important repercussions, the king, Prince Edward and Cornwall's son Henry would remain under some form of restraint; Mortimer, James of Audley and Roger of Leybourne would be granted their liberty. This latter was significant and undermined the baronial triumph of what became known as the Mise of Lewes. Mortimer was an inveterate foe of de Montfort, powerful and energetic: with his power base on the Welsh marches and a large affinity the marcher lord could yet be a prime player in the game, and the game, with Mortimer unfettered, was by no means over.

On 15 May, King Henry III of England handed his regal sword to de Clare; he and his son passed into effective captivity and the reins of government transferred to Simon de Montfort. It was the earl's greatest triumph but it was neither unconditional nor perfect. The earl would find that the winning of power came easier than its retention, that his freeing of the Marchers was most dangerous and that his subsequent failure to submit the Provisions of Oxford to review, as he had undertaken, would be a curse that came back to haunt him. The campaign and Battle of Lewes were done, but the battle for England was just beginning.

The Almonry. This monastic survivor now houses an information centre and battle room. The building is almost in period and the staff are most friendly and helpful – the obvious starting point for a battlefield perambulation.

St Lawrence's Church. The nineteenth-century stained glass window in the north aisle repays study, and the Abbey Park marks the muster point for the Montfortians on the morning of the battle; from here they marched uphill along the line of the present High Street toward Green Hill.

The Abbey Tower. This survives (altered since the thirteenth century) in the Abbey Park in the centre of the modern town. From here it is said de Montfort's barber first sighted the royalist advance to the east. There are some very good interpretation panels which show the extent of the complex as it would have stood prior to the Reformation. The de Montfort memorial stands nearby.

Green Hill, looking eastwards toward the field. Here the slope levels out towards the plateau of Green Hill; the Squires is ahead and to the left. Edward's division would have been deployed on the left and de Clare's on the right. Roughly from this point the Montfortians would have seen the royalist line, and even those who had not fully considered the odds would have drawn breath.

Green Hill, looking westwards back towards the town. It was up the line of the present High Street that de Montfort's knights rode on the day of the battle. The town now extends much further eastwards: this would have been open ground in the thirteenth century, small fields and orchards.

The Leicester Tower. Built by Edward Rudge in 1842, the tower represents the Victorian perception, in the wake of the Great Reform Act of 1832, of de Montfort as a champion of democracy. An embattled octagonal building faced with stone around a brick core, overlooking the Avon, it is said to be based on Guy's Tower at Warwick Castle. It is sited west of the Abbey Manor, some distance from the field.

The Leicester Tower commemorative plaque. 'This Tower was erected in the year MDCCCXLII (1842) to the memory of Simon de Montfort Earl of Leicester the father and founder of the British House of Commons who was slain at the Battle of Evesham in the year MCCLXV (1265).'

THIS TOWER WAS ERECTED
IN THE YEAR MDCCCXLII (1842)
TO THE MEMORY OF
SIMON-DE-MONTFORT
EARL OF LEICESTER
THE FATHER AND FOUNDER OF
THE BRITISH HOUSE OF COMMONS
WHO WAS SLAIN
AT THE BATTLE OF EVESHAM
IN THE YEAR MCCLXV (1265)

The Obelisk, north panel. This relief features ten lines from the 22nd song of Drayton's Polyolbion of 1622, with two new lines added (Cox, *Battle of Evesham*, citing British Archaeological Association Journal, XXXII, p. 79).

The Obelisk, east panel. 'I am Henry of Winchester your King: Do not kill me.' A rather fanciful interpretation of the moment the king is rescued on the field. Both he and his rescuer are portrayed in harness that might look rather better on stage!

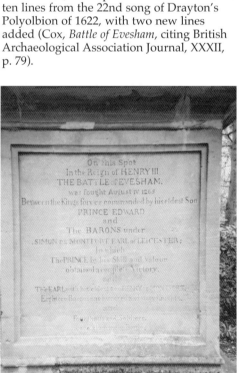

The Obelisk, south panel. 'On this spot in the reign of Henry III the Battle of Evesham was fought August iv 1265 …' The degree of precision is, of course, erroneous.

The Obelisk, west panel. A decorative fan of arms and armorial trappings, perhaps linking the imperial glories of Victoria to the beginnings of parliamentary democracy.

The obelisk viewed from the north. Rudge also erected the pleasingly proportioned obelisk, now obscured by planting. It is on a rise looking eastwards toward Battle Well (470 yards). There was a nineteenth-century belief that Prince Edward's force had deployed on this ground and the fight had occurred in the shallow depression just below.

The field, viewed from the Squires. This is looking south and east from the Squires to the centre of the field where de Montfort's column collided with the royalist line. The ground is now under the plough and bisected by the modern road. In 1265 it would have been open heath.

View of the Downs above Lewes. A general view showing the rolling terrain; though now more cultivated and enclosed it has not changed greatly.

View of the Downs. A further view showing the high ground above the town and looking over the town and castle which is just visible on the right.

Modern Lewes. A view of the townscape, showing how the modern town has swelled beyond the medieval boundaries.

The barbican. The castle barbican viewed from the main street next to the present museum: this is closer to the heart of the bustling medieval town.

View through the barbican, taken looking though the gateway, giving an impression of the narrowness of the town's medieval thoroughfares through which the fighting surged.

View of the castle. The motte and bailey form of construction is plainly visible. This shows the castle's strong position: we can appreciate how formidable an obstacle it was and why no serious attempt was undertaken against it by the Montfortians.

View of the field from the castle. The green space to the left is the Paddock where Edward's cavalry mustered; the hollow behind the houses lying beyond is the Wallands, scene of the clash with the Londoners. Atop the ridge to the right is the grandstand; the bulk of de Montfort's forces were arrayed on the slope to the left.

View from the castle, from the castle walls looking up toward the Downs.

Two views of the ruins of St Pancras' Priory. The ruins belie the extent of the priory complex as it would have appeared in the thirteenth century; much of the site is now under the railway line and the houses lying to the north.

Chapter 5

Evesham (1) – The Campaign

*On the whole, the campaign is the most brilliant piece of medieval
generalship which we have yet to record.*

Sir Charles Oman

The baronial triumph at Lewes was surely God's
vindication of the righteousness of their cause, as the
Franciscan author of *The Song of Lewes* exulted; God 'was
on the side of justice'.[1] God had therefore decided, in the supreme
test of battle, to uphold the Provisions of Oxford and curb the
royal prerogative accordingly. Henry's right to deal with his
kingdom as though it was a mere private estate and without
consultation with his senior magnates was curtailed. Simon's
piety and steadfast adherence to his earlier oath had brought this
to pass; 'the faith and fidelity of Simon alone is become the
security of the peace of all England'.[2] Simon's contacts with the
upper echelons of the clergy served him well; Oxford University,
whose functioning had been rudely interrupted by the royal
muster, was reconvened. Intellectual support was most useful, but
the co-operation of the magnates was essential. We have already
observed that, in de Montfort's complex personal make-up, piety
and self-interest combined; whilst the former might excite the
admiration of senior clergy, the latter alarmed his fellow barons.
However, the earl had the king, Prince Edward, Richard of
Cornwall, his son Henry of Almain and numerous others

completely in his power; by the stroke of Lewes he had emasculated the royalist faction and corralled its leaders.

The constitution

De Montfort had control of the royal seal: this, combined with physical control of the king's person, endowed him with the keys of authority – yet he was not king; he had taken up arms in the name and cause of a constitutional settlement but was perilously close to assuming the role of dictator. Nor was he unchallenged: one of the failures, from his perspective, of the Mise of Lewes was that the terms did not restrain the marcher lords, inveterate foes, who were left to create whatever mayhem they chose in their wide domains. Northern magnates, such as John Baliol, had also been let off the leash, so the north was scarcely more secure – a whole slew of castles, including, at the outset, Windsor and Nottingham, still held out for the king, and these garrisons could not be swiftly eliminated. In the west Bristol and, to the east, Pevensey stubbornly held out; de Valence, Bigod and Guy de Lusignan decamped to France, where they could be certain of a friendly reception from King Louis IX – kings, on the whole, do not like rebels and kingmakers.

Thus, Simon faced opposition from the north and west, and the necessity of protracted siege operations and the very real threat of an external invasion, sponsored by France and orchestrated by Queen Eleanor. If this was not sufficient, the treasury was bare and the recent hostilities had, as an inevitable corollary to civil strife, unleashed a host of disturbances. The collapse of the civil administration hampered Simon's efforts to restore order, as private grudges fanned a spate of minor conflagrations across the troubled shires. On 4 June, in an effort to stem the rising tide of disorder, designated 'keepers of the peace' were appointed for each county; these were quasi-military appointments distinct from the sheriffs whose role continued as before; in some instances these new appointments did more to spread than curb the mischief.[3] In reality Simon's regime could be maintained only by force since the king and prince were effectively hostages and their faction, if temporarily cowed, was by no means willing.

De Montfort had intended that effectively holding hostage the king and prince could provide adequate leverage for Louis IX to agree to a further round of arbitration, as provided for by the Mise of Lewes; yet French acquiescence was not forthcoming. In the end, the very status of the captives implied that no direct action against them could be taken; by the same token any fetters were removed from the marcher lords who could be certain even a de Montfort would not dare lay violent hands upon the Lord's anointed. Despite these difficulties the earl proposed to summon a parliament in late June – the first such assembly since October 1263. Parliament could give constitutional approval to the provisions of the Mise of Lewes and provide a more secure base for de Montfort's tenure. It was none too soon; distinct rumblings could be heard across the Channel and the marchers remained pointedly aloof. On 23 June, Henry, doubtless with bad grace, gave authority for a council of nine senior representatives from the magnates and clergy to be set up; the three men empowered to choose, and whose grant was confirmed by Parliament, were de Montfort, de Clare and Stephen Bersted.

These councillors were, with the king, to have control of the reins of government but Henry, in reality, was reduced to a mere cipher. The resulting ordinance was a bitter pill for the captive king to swallow and was accepted only under duress – the document echoed the Provisions of Oxford, and Simon was its principal architect and author; in this he had fulfilled his earlier vow. However, the authority conferred by the ordinance was now in the hands of a triumvirate rather than the fifteen proposed in 1258; in practical terms it conferred dictatorial status on Simon – the result was more junta than council. Whilst it was understood that this narrow base of emergency powers entrusted to so few hands was to be a temporary expedient pending resolution of the outstanding matters left over from the Mise, these showed no signs of going away. The ordinance could easily be viewed as recognition that the earl had no intention of adhering to the terms of the Mise; this smacked of tyranny and raised hackles throughout the English polity.

Despite the overtones of autocracy Simon went to some lengths to secure wide support for the ordinance which, at best, shifted power completely toward his own faction; nonetheless Parliament, summoned for 24 June, was intended to be widely representative, with four knights from each shire attending. With the approval of such a broad constituency the de Montfortian faction gained a wider measure of credibility; Parliament set the legislative seal upon that which had been gained on the field of battle, conferring the approval of magnates, clergy and gentry. With his constitutional position secure, Simon, aided by de Clare, embarked upon a summer campaign against the troublesome marchers. A swift chevauchee, liberal application of sword and torch, soon brought Mortimer and his allies to their knees; terms were agreed, castles would be handed over and hostages given – this seemed like a further triumph, but the effects were largely illusory.

Whilst Simon was engaged in the west his presence was urgently required in the south-east, where an invasion from the Low Countries appeared imminent: Queen Eleanor, with energy and skill, had brought into being a mercenary army, stiffened by the exiles, and appeared poised to strike. De Montfort riposted by summoning the feudal levy to guard the shores and invoking all possible diplomatic measures to forestall an attack. Simon was magnificent under pressure, and it was undoubtedly his inspirational leadership which held the baronial faction together and which was able to confront two distinct threats on opposing fronts; his biographer eulogizes sufficiently to confer Churchillian status on the earl.[4] Throughout the high summer and autumn of 1264 tortuous and tense negotiations were entered into, aimed at diffusing the external threat: in one sense the fact that the immediate danger was coming from across the Channel played to the English propensity for xenophobia, and united all classes behind de Montfort.

On 15 August fresh terms were dispatched to the French court, those of the Mise of Lewes being unacceptable; these new proposals, known as the Peace of Canterbury, were scarcely more palatable. The June ordinance was reiterated, with all of its limitations on the king's freedoms; the power of the councillors (the three and the nine) was to continue until such time as the provisions of the Mise were fully carried through or, should this not occur, then for the remainder of Henry's life and enduring for an indeterminate period into the reign of his successor. It was one thing to shackle the ageing king (then 57), but another to then fix the same constraints onto his son. In tandem with these stern provisions the church would be reformed, and aliens excluded from high office; previous statutes, including Magna Carta, were to be adhered to. The crown would issue an amnesty to all who had taken the barons' part. Louis found these terms even harder to swallow than the last and reacted angrily – he would accept no provision that so fettered the exercise of kingly authority; it was probably naïve to have expected any other response.

This placed the barons in some difficulties; the senior clergy were already under pressure from the papal legate. The next move represented a more conciliatory approach and, as such, a political rebuff for Simon whose position, as ever, was by no means secure. This plan, however, came to nothing and was in turn replaced by the return to a more hard-line stance. Faced with the opposition of both Louis and the papal legate it is hardly surprising that the barons wavered. On 24 September a strong delegation crossed the Channel to meet with the legate at Boulogne, where they were treated to a reminder as to the extent of the latter's commission; thus harangued the English began to hesitate and offer concessions, though both clergy and lay magnates stood firm in insisting on restraints on the king's power. Threat of excommunication hung in the air, a most powerful incentive. In England Simon temporized and a diplomatic response was sent, but this failed to satisfy the queen, anxious to procure the liberty of her husband and eldest son.

His patience running low, the legate responded with the full arsenal of his office and such a broadside, threatening excommunication and interdict, was bound to be heeded; in essence he demanded an early acceptance that he should act as arbitrator on the whole matter and that an exchange of castles and hostages be agreed. These terms, despite the weight of papal authority, were summarily rejected; the barons were not for moving. The sentences were then broadcast but in Flanders and not in England; for the moment, the game was mired in stalemate. Despite this it was Simon who probably came off worse; the bishops, however ardent their support for reform, could not easily set themselves up against the authority of the papal legate: their position was a most unenviable one, placed between two such opposing poles.

This fear of foreign invasion had been the mortar that cemented the baronial cause in the summer but, once the immediate threat of invasion receded, cracks inevitably reappeared. Simon, of course, was wedded to the June settlement and could not, with ease, withdraw. In one area the interests of the earl and the bishops coincided – the urgent need for reform of the church, which had been subject to many abuses from within and without: de Clare was a prime exponent of such despoliation. Autumn gales blew away the lingering fears of invasion and the papal legate's authority lapsed with the death of Pope Urban IV in October. Any collective sigh of baronial relief would, however, have been premature.

Once more attention shifted to the west, where the restless marcher lords, uncowed by their previous drubbing, were again active. They were joined by a cadre of Prince Edward's mesnie knights who took Bristol and, in early October, went on the offensive, sitting down before de Clare's castle at Hantley in Worcestershire. In November the marchers, not to be outdone, took up Hereford and captured Gloucester, Bridgnorth and, dangerously, Marlborough. The queen may have been in touch with her son's household men who staged a daring, if unsuccessful, raid on Wallingford, where the prince was held. De Montfort transferred high-ranking captives to the safer custody of his fortress at Kenilworth and, once again, took the field against the marchers in the dismal closing days of November. Though they broke down the Severn bridges the earl was able to execute a pincer movement in concert with his Welsh ally Llywelwyn, and the dissidents were obliged to submit at Worcester. An arrangement was hammered out which involved temporary exile for the marchers, some distribution of estates and a possible release of Prince Edward. Simon had again demonstrated his mastery in the field; had, for a second time, trounced the marchers; had defused the external threat and now appeared in an impregnable position. The northerners, seeing which way the wind was blowing, backed off from any confrontation, and important holds, such as Nottingham and Scarborough, Newcastle and Carlisle, still in royalist hands, opened their gates.

Parliament reconvened in January 1265 and remained sitting till the middle part of March; this was the first which involved both the knights of the shires and the urban bourgeoisie. One of the principal matters was the mechanism for securing Prince Edward's release. A separate agenda revolved around the garnering of riches by de Montfort and his family; Simon's supremacy allowed full rein to his avarice, one of his prominently unattractive characteristics. Such venality was scarcely unknown and high office was frequently viewed as a passport to wealth. Simon was distinguished by the zeal with which he pursued his family's interest, garnering a share of the spoils that left numerous of his supporters feeling disadvantaged. Richard of Cornwall's lands proved particularly attractive – the earl was vastly wealthy and none of the previous discussions led to or even appeared to contemplate his early release. There was policy in this as well as greed: de Montfort had achieved and maintained his dominance by force of arms, and cash was needed to pay the broadswords which maintained that position. On the earl's subsequent death in battle at Evesham his widow fled to France, taking her late husband's war chest which still bulged with the very considerable amount of 11,000 marks.[5] De Montfort has always been considered a good general, and rightly so, but now stuffed with ransoms and the wealth of forfeited estates, he was also a very rich one.

Simon continued to exhibit this strange and, to us, alien mix of absolute piety and notorious avarice; the monarch was reduced to the status of an impecunious pensioner, but herein lay the seeds of nemesis: who was truly king – was it Henry or 'King' Simon; had the barons drawn steel simply to replace one tyrant with another? For as long as the threat posed by the marchers in the west and the exiles in Flanders remained potent, Simon was indispensable – his failings simply had to be tolerated, as there was no other who could lead as well as he. When the threats receded but the acquisitiveness did not, rumblings quickly spilled into dangerous divisions. De Montfort had fallen into the trap of concentrating largesse on too narrow an affinity, his own; powerful allies such as de Clare and John Giffard swiftly came to resent this, and Simon lacked that finesse which could empower him to heal rifts. The level of defections in terms of numbers was small, but the consequences were very considerable – a man in Simon's fragile position could ill afford to alienate so great a magnate as de Clare: to do so was rank folly, the pinnacle of hubris – 'The pride of arrogant Lucifer'.[6]

One way of buying popular support from the gentry was to offer relief on loans – this was also, from Simon's point of view, remarkably cost-effective, as the burden was borne by Jewish money-lenders who held the security. Simon was, as we have seen, notably anti-Semitic in an age known for its intolerance. Moves such as this and the summoning of Parliament at the start of 1265 may be viewed as attempts to win support on the back of the continuing reform agenda; those who attended, from the magnates downward, were carefully sifted, and the clergy were present in large numbers. Though he was autocratic in manner and bearing de Montfort was not a dictator; rather he was the supreme head of a narrow oligarchy, which, lacking widespread magnatial support, sought to bolster its position by appealing to a far wider constituency and capitalizing on relations with the church. The earl could, perhaps disingenuously, argue that, by taking into his own hands so many pilfered estates, he was merely securing the power base he needed from which to pursue, successfully, the reform agenda.

De Montfort's regime
If King Henry had been reduced to a mere cipher, his son certainly had not; Prince Edward was now the focus for any

resurgence in royalist activity. The barons and de Montfort could not hold the heir to the throne captive indefinitely: a compromise was needed which would give the prince his freedom and yet guarantee the reformers' agenda. Both the negotiations and accompanying proposals proved complex, but, by 10 March, Edward had indicated that a consensus was at hand. This was more artifice than settlement, for the king's ability to rule was still to be determined by the conciliar provisions of the earlier ordinance, and Prince Edward was subject to sufficient constraints as to make the difference between freedom and captivity virtually undetectable. The March arrangement thus sought to continue a level of restraint on the exercise of the royal prerogative which far exceeded that envisaged by the Provisions of Oxford. The earl was taking under his own hand Chester, the Peak and Newcastle, and though lands were to be provided in exchange he was alienating Edward from a substantial slice of his appenage, in terms of annual income perhaps a quarter of the whole. These holdings came to de Montfort in fee, so could be passed on whilst the property offered in exchange could not be compared in value. This was a very considerable step and transferred great power to the earl whilst, at the same time, considerably reducing the estate of the heir to the throne; for critics this was indeed rampant and dangerous hubris.

Another magnate and something of a loose cannon was Robert de Ferrers, youthful Earl of Derby, who had previously been significantly at odds with the prince. During the Lewes campaign Edward had taken up his enemy's lands with gusto, a favour returned with interest once Longshanks was corralled. Derby had assumed de facto control of much of the territory Simon was now seeking to enter. Ferrers was at best a lukewarm supporter of de Montfort, and by February 1265 was enjoying a sojourn in the Tower. Simon, as ever, was saddled with a large brood for which he had to provide; his venality thus extended to two generations, and his ascendancy helped establish his sons in a style that would never otherwise have been possible. If he saw the danger signs in this, as surely he must have done, he ignored them. His eldest lads, Henry and Simon, did very well, as did their younger siblings,

Guy and Amaury, if to a lesser extent. The father's largesse placed the sons in strategically significant holdings and increased the power-base of his affinity; his daughter, Eleanor, was promised to Prince Llywelwyn.[7] The younger de Montforts were as unscrupulously avaricious as their father. Simon junior ruthlessly oppressed his enemy William de Braose; the latter, a royalist, had taken up one of Simon's manors in Sussex; in June 1264 a partisan and drumhead tribunal fined the absent de Braose a huge sum by way of compensation. The whole shabby process was no more than a tool for further sequestration.

Such blatant plundering and the summary incarceration of the Earl of Derby served to create a disastrous rift with de Clare. Private grievance sharpened the policy divide which deepened after Lewes. De Clare wished to see the royalist hostages released; de Montfort felt more secure otherwise. De Clare also was emerging as the true champion of the Provisions of Oxford: he was alienated by de Montfort's reliance on mercenaries and by the ruthless advancement of his own sons for whom Gloucester had little time. With Ferrers gaoled de Clare might easily have shivered, fearing he must be next; perhaps he was nothing more than an impediment to the further enrichment of Simon and his heirs. His comrade-in-arms had become the very authoritarian figure the Provisions of Oxford sought to contain. A more subtle man than Simon would have taken steps, indeed gone to considerable lengths, to placate so powerful an ally. Particularly he would have more effectively curbed his sons' intemperate hostility toward de Clare. These two sets of mettlesome and proud young men had been due to meet at a joust planned for Dunstable on 17 February, but Simon called the whole business off, fearing that hot tempers might lead to real rather than sham fighting.[8]

Gloucester now withdrew into the west, finding it convenient to pursue his quarrel with the Welsh; Llywelwyn had been raiding his lands and the prince was, of course, an ally of de Montfort's. Simon had now fallen into the pit his own overweening hubris had dug: he had alienated his principal magnatial ally, an outcome which a regime as narrowly based as his could ill afford. A more cautious and subtle man would have either avoided such a breach or moved swiftly to repair; John Giffard, another key supporter, had already defected. Simon's sons, by their arrogance and propensity toward the use of force, were proving highly detrimental to their father's fragile regime. Gloucester's alienation was most telling, as he was the junta's one major prop on the Welsh marches, where so many enemies lurked; losing him created an axis of opposition which would prove much the harder to contain.

At a time when he should have been anxious to placate de Clare, Simon compounded the rift by demanding return of Bamburgh, that distant and lordly fortress, seat of the ancient Northumbrian kings; Gloucester's garrison demurred. Parliament rose in mid-March, and by the 19th de Montfort had journeyed to his manor of Odiham, a brief interlude of calm in the storm that was poised to erupt. As the Dunstable joust had been postponed, it was now proposed to break a few lances at Northampton on 20 April. De Clare wisely stayed away, and Simon kept the king and Prince Edward close. The mood was febrile; spring brought no relief from the clouds amassing over the troubled edifice of de Montfort's regime. Suspicions festered, and John fitz Alan, who, as lord of Clun in Shropshire and of Arundel in Sussex, held important castles in the two most critical regions, was required either to surrender the latter or provide his son as hostage. In the final week of April, de Montfort, with his immediate affinity, took the fateful road west, arriving at Gloucester on the 27th. Simon was, of course, aware that he once again faced danger, but he would not, at this stage, have believed he was undertaking his final, disastrous campaign.

The campaign of Evesham
That the situation in the west was difficult, perhaps even critical, was obvious; still, the earl had both king and prince, to all intents and purposes hostages, in his train. De Clare might be disaffected but had shown no immediate signs of raising a large force of marchers; he was building his numbers, to be sure, but de Montfort had travelled this road before, and had forced these troublesome lords to bend their knee on every occasion. He had

his household men around him and probably a substantial mercenary corps; it was a time of caution rather than outright alarum. His son Henry rode with him, as did other key magnates, Peter de Montfort, Giles D'Argentan, Roger de St John and Humphrey Bohun, all members of the council of nine. He could also count upon Hugh Despenser and John fitz John. The south-east was controlled by the younger Simon with such staunch allies as Richard de Grey and Adam of Newmarket; the regime still seemed very much in control.

Gloucester, as a base for offensive operations, had something of the feel of a salient. Whilst no hostile forces yet ringed this key bastion, the buzz of discontent seemed to resonate through the warm spring air. Giffard and Gloucester had indeterminate forces nearby; Mortimer lurked in his fortress of Wigmore to the north-west, whilst, south and west, Edward's household men from Bristol forayed unchallenged. The earl, with customary zeal, summoned the county levies from Gloucestershire, Worcestershire and Herefordshire to muster at Hereford and then concentrate upon Gloucester. Such warlike preparations were accompanied by a bout of diplomacy whereby Simon sought terms with de Clare. Neither party wished for an outright return to hostilities, so a compromise agreement was entered into on 12 May. This provided that their political and personal differences should be settled by arbitration, though the men chosen to carry out this review were markedly pro-Montfortian. It is possible de Clare was not unduly concerned; his words were intended to buy time rather than concessions for, even as he talked, both de Valence and de Warenne landed in Pembrokeshire with their affinities – the exiles had returned, with swords drawn.

It is not possible to say whether, at this time, the various disaffected elements had achieved any degree of cohesion or if the landings were carefully timed – that a concerted plan existed cannot be ruled out, however. In any event this fresh development was most serious from Simon's perspective; it cannot be coincidental that the lordship of Pembroke was held by de Clare and that his entering into negotiations might be nothing more than a ruse. As ever the earl reacted with vigour, marching his

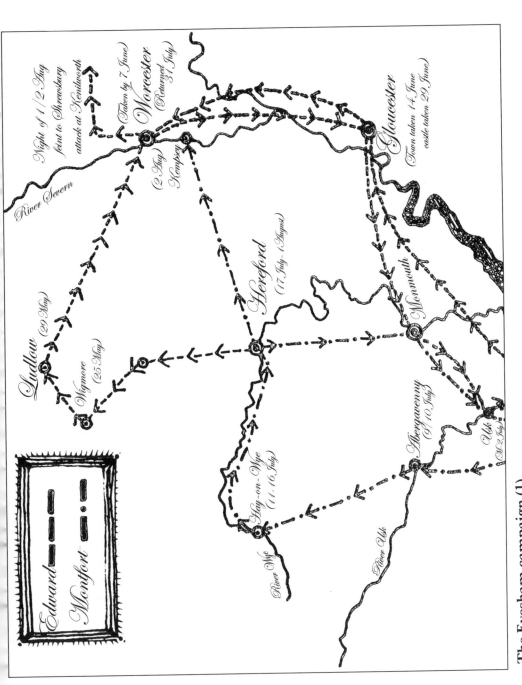

The Evesham campaign (1)

available forces to Hereford, where he was well placed to create a buffer between de Clare, the exiles and Mortimer at Wigmore. Simon could now have little doubt that he was facing a major threat and a renewal of the armed struggle. He pressed on with his plans to summon a parliament for 1 June; nonetheless the scale of preparations being undertaken at Hereford clearly suggests he was planning a new offensive against the enemies gathering, like circling sparrowhawks, around him.

May 28th was to prove a key date in the course of the campaign: on the very day de Montfort was greeting the abbot of Chester and usurping the prince's lands, Edward himself contrived to escape his clutches. This was not a spontaneous dash but the successful outcome of careful planning. Gloucester's men were just beyond Hereford's walls and de Clare's brother Thomas, in whom de Montfort continued to trust, was the facilitator. On the day the prince, with Thomas de Clare, escorted by a squadron of baronial horse, rode out ostensibly to test the mettle of his horses. Having swapped mounts as his own tired after the gallops, the prince spurred for freedom on the only fresh horse remaining. Thomas de Clare and a handful of defectors straggled after him. All evaded their erstwhile captors.

At Wigmore, Longshanks met firstly with Mortimer and then with de Clare at Ludlow: terms were swiftly negotiated, both men needing an early accord. Edward undertook to prevail upon the king, his father, to govern in accordance with custom and, tellingly, to expel all foreigners from his service. By this means Edward established a manifesto which undercut Simon's – he was promising to undertake that which de Montfort had himself promised but had failed to deliver, compromising the integrity of his position with some blatant and unbridled self-interest. Simon's venality and that of his sons was proving his undoing, uniting the opposition and undermining the vestiges of authority still clinging to his tottering regime. From the earl's perspective the situation had passed beyond serious: it was now potentially deadly.

Perhaps the telling difference between the campaigns of Lewes and Evesham is the fact that the royalists, this time led by Edward, controlled the strategy of the preliminary moves and then determined the course of the final battle; Evesham, in some ways, was the reverse of Lewes. Simon seems to have struggled throughout – he was indifferently served by his sons and finally humbugged by the prince. De Montfort never gave way to doubt or to despair: true to his combative and confident nature, he strove till the last; he failed to rate as a general of the first rank, unlike Longshanks, but as a leader of men he remained inspirational to the very end. Even with defeat and death staring him in the face, he did not waver but rode out toward his final battle with that degree of sangfroid which was the badge of the true knight. For all his faults, Simon never failed as a man.

Edward now moved swiftly to contain Simon west of the great river barrier of the Severn. The earl was considering a muster at Worcester for 30 May, but a week later this prospect had vanished. The prince had secured the city and slighted the key bridge spanning the broad course of the river. Undaunted, Simon prepared to switch to Gloucester, still a vital bastion, now more so than ever, and one where castle and crossing were strongly posted. He still believed he could wrest back the initiative and was, even on 12 June, issuing summonses to various parties to attend the king at Gloucester; by the 19th he had negotiated an alliance with Llywelwyn, thus both securing the far western flank and adding a Welsh corps to his army. This seemed to augur well, but Glasbury, where terms with the Welsh were agreed, was 50 miles west of Gloucester which, by 14 June, was already under attack, with the royalists quickly gaining possession of the streets, though the castle still held firm.

This development did open out certain possibilities for the Montfortians. Edward had the very considerable advantage of operating, at this point, on interior lines; his enemies were not united and he was well placed to deal with each in turn. Should, however, the baronial forces be able to unite – they, of course, were relying on exterior lines – then their combined forces would outmatch those of the royalists. Gloucester could be the fulcrum where the prince's army was crushed between hammer and anvil. Simon hurrying eastwards from Hereford could expect Simon the

Younger to strike westwards. A major flaw in any such manoeuvre was the fact that castle and town were on the east not the west bank; young Simon was bogged down in the fruitless siege of Pevensey and was to display little of his father's élan in marching westwards; as the royalists marched into Gloucester his army was most likely no further west than London. On 29 June the castellan at Gloucester struck his colours and the vital bridge, soon cast down, came under royalist control; de Montfort was now penned west of the Severn. First honours to Prince Edward.

Simon was far from beaten. With Gloucester written off and no signs of his tardy offspring, the earl around 24 June had decided on a bold strategy: he would now march south from Hereford to Monmouth, and from there reach Newport and the Bristol Channel and escape the net by ship. This was logical as well as bold, but the march was delayed by a royalist force under John Giffard at Monmouth; with the crossing there strongly posted Simon concluded he could not easily force a passage. He had next to fight for possession of de Clare's castle at Usk which, though it did not hold out for long, delayed the baronial army to the extent that it was 4 July before Simon's forces could enter Newport. Matters were not going according to plan. Usk had fallen, as had Abergavenny, and, bolstered by his Welsh spears, Simon took up de Clare's lands around; Sir Charles Oman believes this was no random chevauchee but an attempt to force de Clare to respond, drawing him westwards and leaving the road from London clear for Simon the Younger.

Though the royalists held the castle, the citizens of Bristol were well enough disposed towards the baronial faction to heed Simon's request for ships to be dispatched over to Newport. Prince Edward was hard on his heels, and Usk was retaken after a bare couple of days and Giffard's force brought in. Simon's plans now began very swiftly to unravel. Edward had learnt of the plan for ships from Bristol and had ordered a cutting-out expedition comprising a trio of galleys found at Gloucester. These were crewed by chosen men and came up just as the baronial ships were gliding into Newport harbour, having already begun the job of loading supplies. A fierce little action on the water now began, with the royalists quickly gaining the upper hand; nearly a dozen baronial vessels were taken or sent to the bottom of the channel. This was bad; worse, the royalists were snapping at Simon's heels outside the town, on the east bank of the Usk. Wisely the earl decided this was not the place for a general engagement: he caused the bridge to be burnt, thus securing his rear, and on 7 July slipped clear of the town with all his power. He had survived, but the strategic initiative lay with the royalists.

For Simon, pushed ever westwards and away from his son's forces, the only recourse now was to regain Hereford by a series of forced marches. Having abandoned Newport, the army marched the 17 miles to Abergavenny (via Pontypool, bypassing Usk). On 11 July, in broiling heat, they covered another 28 miles to attain Hay-on-Wye. This was a particularly trying march: the weather was hot and dry, provisions were scarce and they had to overcome the obstacle of barren high ground, the formidable Black Mountains. Morale cannot have been high, and even the meanest footslogger would have divined that matters were going badly and they had been harried from pillar to post by the superior royalists. The English toiling through this Welsh landscape chafed at the unfamiliar diet of mutton and milk, missing their habitual bread ration.[9] Carpenter places the baronial army back within Hereford by 16 July, whilst Oman puts their arrival as no sooner than the 20th – we can be sure that the exhausted troops were to remain there until 1 August, although some did reach as far north as Leominster, where the royalist garrison was captured.[10]

Despite these reverses and privations the strategic position was not much altered; true, Edward had kept his enemies behind the formidable barrier of the Severn, but he had to be wary of the very real risk that he might yet be trapped between the two baronial armies. Various eminent authors, including Oman and Burne, have found little good to say about Simon the Younger, criticizing him for a slow and circuitous approach. Carpenter takes a less pejorative view, and points out that Simon the Younger posed a sufficient threat to draw Prince Edward back to his former base of Worcester. The younger Simon had reached Winchester from London some time between 14 and 16 July – had his father succeeded in reaching Bristol then this would have made sense; obviously that was not possible and the son thoroughly took up Winchester before marching on to Oxford. Here he remained for three days, again not necessarily without purpose; he may have been seeking to ascertain if Gloucester could be attempted. If this was contemplated it was decided against: the city could not be easily retaken nor the Severn crossing opened up. He next moved to Northampton, possibly taking this rather longer route to minimize risk of ambush, and reached Kenilworth by 31 July.

Kenilworth

The younger Simon may not have matched his father's vigour on the march to Kenilworth, but it would be reasonable to surmise that contact was at some point established; Evesham does appear to have been chosen as the hub of concentration.[11] This was eminently sensible, for the town was mid-way between the two forces. From there, two major arterial routes led from Worcester, the royalists' base, toward London and Oxford. If Edward wanted to break out of the west to march south and east then Evesham was the obvious starting point. With the Montfortians concentrated there, they were well placed to offer battle on equal terms. By dusk on the last day in July the baronial forces at Kenilworth were taking their ease; if their marches had been less strenuous, both men and horses would be tired and in need of some recuperation. Simon the Younger did not apparently consider that he might be attacked, and his precautions were somewhat lax. This was to prove disastrous.

Altogether, the host was too large to be easily accommodated within the sheltering walls of the great fortress, so many were billeted more comfortably in the town, some in the timber-framed houses, others under canvas; Simon himself, with some of his affinity, took lodgings within the priory, perhaps the plum billet. Whilst guards were posted, none in the army appeared fearful of surprise; some accounts suggest that liquor flowed liberally, Simon and other lords retiring somewhat unsteadily to their beds.[12] One of the most tantalizing aspects of medieval warfare is that we learn little from the chroniclers about intelligence. Armies employed spies, of course, but Prince Edward appears singularly well served, far more so than his enemies, and the night action which ensued is a textbook example of the inestimable worth of sound and reliable intelligence. One of Simon's household men, Ralph of Arden, was an Edwardian agent; his accomplice, known as Margot, presumably young and boyish, was able to slip out of Kenilworth in the guise of a page and alert the royalists at Worcester. Prince Edward thus gained an invaluable insight into his enemy's present dispositions and the plan for a rendezvous at Evesham on 4 August.

Longshanks was not one to let such a golden opportunity pass, and he resolved upon a major spoiling raid against Simon the Younger's forces massed at Kenilworth. Beating up enemy quarters is a high-risk strategy, requiring boldness, dash and a fair measure of luck. Edward, however, now knew two things vital for success: one, his enemies were unprepared, and, two, their forces were dispersed through the town and he knew precisely where each of the rebel officers was billeted – no need, then, for carnage; surgery would do rather better. He immediately summoned his forces to march. Wary of Montfortian spies in his own ranks he gave out the plan was a northward movement aimed at Bridgnorth, Shrewsbury or Stafford; the roads to all three passed through Kidderminster. Edward did not turn left as he might have done but forked right at Barbourne, barely a mile outside Worcester; this road led directly to Kenilworth.

We have to consider the distances involved – from Worcester to Kenilworth is some 34 miles, whilst Hereford lies 27 miles beyond the royalist base; Simon the Elder probably received confirmation of his son's arrival in the course of 1 August. Emboldened, he marched out immediately, probably during the short summer night, and finally managed, after so many marches, to gain the east bank of the Severn. This crossing was managed by Kempsey, barely four miles south of the royalists. Edward, however, was, on the night of the 1st, marching northwards, even as the baronial spies were hurrying to find Simon the Elder, bearing false intelligence. A confusion of sources here obfuscates the likely course of events: as Carpenter observes,[13] Wykes relates that when the royalists resumed their marches in the dark hours of 3–4 August, making for the fateful field of Evesham, they first detoured north for several miles to create a false impression. The Evesham Chronicle provides a more believable sequence of events: Edward's march toward Shrewsbury was the curtain-raiser for his attack on Kenilworth on the evening of the 1st. Evesham states that the foot and baggage accompanied the cavalry but that the latter took the fork to Kenilworth whilst the foot, having achieved their purpose, were not engaged.

This must surely be correct: given the distance, a foot column could not possibly cover so much ground in one night, fight a battle and then return the next day; it was no mean feat for a mounted column. Sir Charles Oman is of the view that the subsequent action in the streets and houses of Kenilworth resulted in significant baronial losses: 'The baronial army was practically annihilated.'[14] This was not in fact the case; Edward was attacking with just a commanded body of horse: this was a commando raid not an offensive, scalpel not sledgehammer. His prime objective was to capture the barons in their beds, and he knew which beds they were in; by taking rather than killing the magnates and gentry he stripped Simon the Younger's army of its officers at a single stroke. As a fighting force this division of the baronial army would be neutralized, rendered impotent. Some of the rebels, targets of opportunity, would be gleefully hacked down in the brief melee, but whatever the loss in men, it was trifling and confined to the commons. Simon still had forces to bring to the field, but Kenilworth defeated the barons' cause as surely as the subsequent denouement at Evesham.

Such gains were by no means certain as Edward's squadrons turned toward their goal. Most probably they were few in number, and thus surprise was of the essence; if this was lost, the whole purpose of the raid was compromised. It was later said that Edward suffered a crisis of confidence at some point and only the bold urging of Roger de Clifford convinced him to steady and continue.[15] Sunrise at that time of year would be around 4.45 am, and the royalists had completed their approach undetected; as their spies had advised, a defile or gully just outside the town provided a convenient lying-up place from which to plan the assault.[16] Most accounts, including both Dr Carpenter's and Dr Cox's, are confident that de Clare, de Valence and Roger Mortimer were with the prince (an alternative view is put forward by Tony Spicer; see Appendix 1). This would be the testing hour: surprise was their ally but the enemy were many, and their horses were very fatigued by the long ride through the summer night. A sudden alarum, the sound of men and harness nearby: for a dread instant it must have seemed they were discovered but not by a baronial army, rather a supply or foraging party, trundling wagons. The whole was captured intact, still without the alarum being raised, and the foragers' fresh mounts provided a welcome boost.[17]

Now was the moment: we may deduce that, as Edward knew the precise identity and location of each of the targets, that small groups would be detailed off as, in the modern idiom, 'snatch squads', whilst the rest stirred the hornets' nest and created a rousing diversion. These squads knew their role, and their objective was to capture, not to kill. In the mid-thirteenth century the town of Kenilworth was grouped around two nodal points, castle and priory; the latter lay south of High Street on the eastern flank, and the ribbon development along that thoroughfare straggled out towards Coventry. Across the Finham Brook, lining the Warwick road, was the other settled area; the stream had previously been dammed to create the broad water defence of the Mere (great pool) and the Lower Pool, then the abbey and town pools south-east of the priory.[18]

Those Montfortians, including the befuddled younger Simon, now experienced a singularly rude awakening as a steel-tipped avalanche of mailed horsemen burst into the streets. From comfortable sleep, arose panic and confusion. Those caught in the wake of the attack mostly fell where they stood. Simon, only half-clothed, bolted for the security of the castle; he was lucky, others were not. If Simon slipped the net, the Earl of Oxford, Gilbert de Gaunt, William de Munchensy, Richard de Grey and his son John, Adam of Newmarket, Baldwin Wake, Walter de Colville and Hugh de Neville were all taken, a full and satisfying bag. Edward wanted captives not corpses, but de Clare insisted on the decapitation of a luckless clerk of the elder Simon's household, Master Stephen of Holwell, dragged from the illusory sanctuary of consecrated ground.[19] The haul comprised not only the prisoners but, apart from the usual booty, a cache of Montfortian banners – these would have a part to play in the greater fight that was looming. Edward had dealt a significant blow to one half of the enemy forces; there now remained the other.

Chapter 6

Evesham (2) – The Battle

*Such was the murder of Evesham,
for battle it was none.*
Robert of Gloucester

E dward's masterly raid on Kenilworth had blunted the
potential thrust from the younger Simon; the father would
be a much tougher nut to crack. De Montfort had incurred
much opprobrium in seeking to provide for his brood: he could
possibly have overcome this had not the sons themselves
exacerbated the problem by flaunting their own hubris. Not only
were they arrogant, they were ruthlessly avaricious and notably
prone to violence. It is said that, on the field of Evesham, as the
baronial army toiled up the slope to its fate, Simon rebuked his
son Henry, accusing him that it was their greed which had
brought about the fall. This may be apocryphal but it has a certain
ring of veracity. The baronial forces had finally crossed the crucial
barrier of the Severn at Clevelode, located in the manor of
Kempsey and owned by a stout Montfortian, Walter de Cantilupe,
Bishop of Worcester.[1]

Advance to contact
As Carpenter points out, there is a measure of confusion as to the
elder Simon's movements in those first, crucial days of August;
Ramsay, Oman and Burne all assert that the earl quit Kempsey on
3 August and marched the dozen and more miles to Evesham that

day. The current view, however, based upon a rereading of the chronicle sources is that the advance to Evesham took place only during the hours of darkness on the night of 3–4 August and that the baronial army arrived at Evesham on the morning of the 4th, just prior to the battle. Cox follows the contemporary view, considering that Simon marched from Kempsey at dusk (say 7.30 pm) and thus reached Evesham just after sunrise (at that time of the year around 4.43 am), certainly before the expiry of the first hour (5.58 am). By the evening of the 3rd the earl would have been aware of his son's difficulties and the success of the royalist descent. He would have viewed this as a setback rather than a disaster; Simon the Younger's army was beaten but not destroyed – he had 'lost not all his power . . . but kept a great host'.[2] There was no reason why he could not lead forces to Evesham for a juncture on the 4th. The town itself would, in any event, be a sensible staging point if de Montfort intended simply to march toward Kenilworth and join his son there.

For the whole of 3 August, then, or at least during the long, hot hours of day, neither army moved. Some writers find this anomalous, and yet, certainly in Edward's case, his men would have desperately needed rest. The foot may not have marched far, but the horse had ridden the hard miles to Kenilworth, fought a sharp little action and then ridden back to Worcester; neither men nor mounts would be immediately ready to deploy again. Edward could derive satisfaction from the knowledge that he had significantly blunted young Simon's spear, but it was not broken; if he could be joined by the earl then the Montfortians would combine into a very substantial army. The royalists had no grounds for complacency – Robert of Gloucester tells us that the army from Kenilworth, their earlier losses notwithstanding, had by the morning of 4 August advanced as far as Alcester, a mere nine miles north of Evesham.[3] One cannot but wonder if, had the younger Simon possessed the drive and energy of his father, matters might still have ended very differently.

Through the short summer night, the heat of day still heavy on dust-laden roads, the baronial army moved; if we assume a marching speed of 2½ mph[4] then reaching Evesham in the first

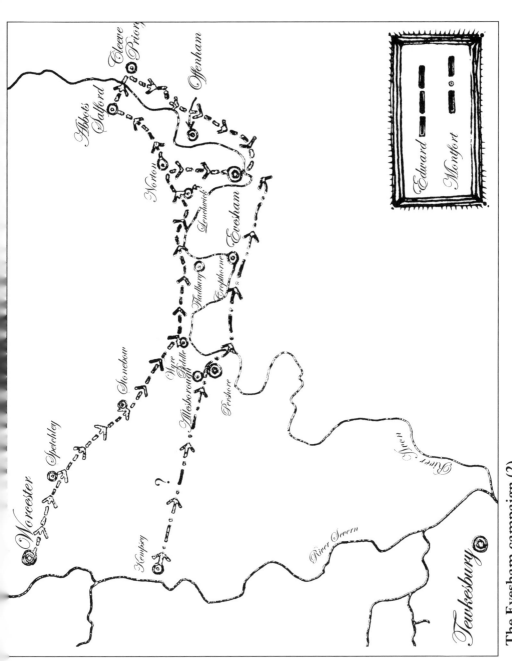

The Evesham camraign (2)

light or morning would be no great hardship. The route would have taken it onto what is now the A44, crossing the Avon firstly at Pershore and then again by the bridge at Evesham, standing south-east of the abbey complex. On reaching the town, Earl Simon, together with the captive king, no better than a recalcitrant mascot, heard early mass and, on Henry's peevish insistence, took some modest refreshment; Simon, unbendingly austere, at first demurred. He had weighty matters on his mind: effecting union with his son's forces was but part of his intention; the rest was to put some ground between himself and the royalists, whom he still believed to be at Worcester. The four miles between there and Kempsey had been far too close for comfort: over the past weeks the morale of his men had been severely tested, and the news from Kenilworth was not calculated to raise the spirits.

Edward had two key objectives, both urgent – he must first prevent a junction of his enemies and, second, he should bring Earl Simon to battle on favourable ground as soon as possible. An advance to Evesham, if properly timed, would place the royalists between the two baronial divisions, thus frustrating a juncture and would, if executed with due swiftness, place them on ground which would facilitate a death blow to the earl's army. Evesham is a pleasant market town; it is remarkable in that it is surrounded on three sides by the Avon, which flows around east, south and west in a loop so that the northern approach, with the ground rising markedly heading out of the town, is the only clear direction of access and egress. It is at the top of the rise that the three roads coming in from Alcester, Worcester and Stratford all join and that into the town descends Green Hill – probably the same line as the present A435 (T). Though no evidence of rig and furrow can be detected, it is possible that the ground was farmed; there is mention of 'East and West fields'. Cox suggests that a straggle of orchards and enclosures surrounded the town and that Green Hill itself with the ground beyond was common pasture, easy ground upon which to deploy troops.

At this time town and abbey were nestled against the head of the loop; the abbey with its attendant parochial chapels was the most distinguished building by far, and parklands stretched down to the river, with the streets concentrated just north of the abbey precincts, around the bridge at Bengeworth; this key crossing was the only means whereby an army could enter the town from the south. If the bridge was sealed off then any defenders within the town would be forced to either defend the place or attempt to break out northwards. As matters stood in the early hours of 4 August, his men having marched all night, Simon, of course, did not intend to fight a battle. He had no aversion to fighting, but the odds would not be even until he had joined his son; for the meantime he had to keep out of reach of the royalists.

Sir Charles Oman accepts that Edward had divided his army into three corps and that these advanced through the hours of darkness on the night of 3–4 August. Oman is content to suggest that by first light they too were approaching Evesham and that the prince came from the north (Worcester–Flyford–Dunnington– Norton); de Clare marched on his right, thus approaching from the north-west (Worcester–Wyre–Craycombe), whilst Mortimer came up on the western flank (Worcester– Pershore–Hampton). The chronicler Trevet tells us Prince Edward marched from Worcester and traversed a river by a settlement he calls 'Clive' – this location has since been associated with Cleeve Prior on the Avon. It lies some fifteen miles east of Worcester and some five miles north-east of Evesham; there was a ford here and the Evesham–Stratford–Kenilworth road runs through it. That the army was divided into three marching corps is supported by Guisborough, Trevet and the Evesham chronicler; the latter confirms that these several axes of advance effectively penned the earl's forces within the town and the encircling loop of the Avon.[5]

The road which passes through Cleeve Prior is that which leads to Kenilworth: by cutting this, therefore, Edward had effectively blocked Earl Simon's route. This presupposes that de Montfort was intending to march on Kenilworth; if his objective was in fact Alcester then this road too would have to be controlled – to cover one and not the other was pointless. It is generally accepted that at or before Cleeve, de Clare's corps was detached to approach Evesham via the Alcester road; common sense would validate this. Wykes, however, offers confirmation when he states that one corps of the royal army was hidden from the eyes of the baronial division in Evesham by rising ground – all concur this must refer to Green Hill.

There is less consensus as to the approach of the third royalist corps under Mortimer and the role the marchers played in the subsequent battle; the debate is somewhat convoluted but is essential to our fuller understanding of the course of the deployment and ensuing combat. It is possible that the prince, having crossed at Cleeve and detached Clare's corps to cover the Alcester road, reached Offenham on the east bank of the Avon, some two miles north of the town – it was here he then detached Mortimer's corps to sweep around to the west and block the exit by securing the bridge at Bengeworth. The prince then used the ford and bridge at Offenham to bring his own corps to the west bank and unite with de Clare.[6] Both Ramsay and Burne take this view, but Carpenter points out that Guisborough, one of our chief sources, is emphatic that, from the defender's perspective, Edward's corps approached from the north, and Mortimer from the west and to the rear.

Sir Charles Oman, however, takes the view that Mortimer's corps was detached from the outset and marched via a different route, actually following that taken by Simon; this is, at least in part, favoured by Carpenter and Tony Spicer, and has much to recommend it. The inherent logic is that though Edward with his own and de Clare's corps had cut both the Kenilworth and Alcester roads, the trap was not fully set unless de Montfort's possible line of escape from the town was also sealed. Had the earl marched from Evesham to the north and found his line of advance checked, he could simply have turned about and escaped south or westwards over the bridge across which he had earlier entered Evesham. This would not have been an easy manoeuvre but it would have been possible; Earl Simon was a general who drilled and trained his men, and Edward knew his formidable uncle should never be underestimated. For present purposes I propose to accept that this was indeed the case (please also refer to Appendix 1, for a further discussion). Carpenter disagrees with

Oman in that he rejects the notion Mortimer was detached from the commencement of the night march. If Edward marched along the Flyford–Dunnington road his army would have been some seven miles to the north of de Montfort's movement along the Pershore–Evesham route. If this was the case, and given that these manoeuvres took place entirely in the dark, neither army could have had any real idea as to the whereabouts of the other.

Carpenter avers that the royalists in fact followed the line of the present B4084.[7] De Montfort, as mentioned, came onto what is now the direction of the A44 just before Pershore. This alternative puts the armies no more than two miles distant and on a parallel course, separated by the river barrier of the Avon. If this was so, and the logic is compelling, then it was at the village of Fladbury that Mortimer's corps was detached; the Avon could be forded at Cropthorne, and Earl Simon's army followed as it entered Evesham. This must surely be the correct interpretation and Oman has not fully considered the difficulties in taking medieval armies over largely unknown roads during darkness. When the royalists left Worcester there was no clear understanding that Evesham was their goal, and to have detached Mortimer at this point would have been tactically unsound. Edward's intention was simple: to shadow and entrap the baronial forces, whilst giving de Montfort no hint of what they were about; if the earl was alerted he could have taken steps to slip the snare that was tightening around him. To succeed Edward must delay that moment of recognition until it was too late to avert the looming catastrophe. In this he was entirely successful.

Once Mortimer had taken the fork at Fladbury, Edward, with his and de Clare's corps, may have quit the line of the B4084 and marched north to cut the Alcester road just short of the hamlet of Norton;[8] de Clare was detached here whilst the prince's corps continued its march for a further distance of $2\frac{1}{2}$ miles to reach Cleeve. Carpenter suggests that using the crossings at Offenham was avoided as this considerably increased the risk of observation, even if, by then, it was barely light; nonetheless the passage of a large number of armed men would have been likely to attract attention in a quiet countryside. Cox prefers to rely on an assertion put forward by the Evesham chronicler that the two corps jointly climbed the rise of Green Hill by a venerable stone marker identified as Siflaed's Stone (see Appendix 2). This stood some 230 yards west of the river Avon immediately north of a trackway (now Blayney's Lane) which leads from the crossing at Offenham to the ridge of Green Hill. Clearly this entry suggests that Edward's corps had used the bridge and ford at Offenham.[9]

We must again focus on the question of numbers and we descend, once more, into the realm of conjecture. Melrose claims that the royalists enjoyed a comfortable superiority, perhaps as high as three to one or more. That the prince commanded a significantly larger army is clear. De Montfort was relying upon the reinforcements being brought by his son and had no intention of giving battle beforehand. His army had endured weeks of hard campaigning and would have suffered reduction through death, wounds, sickness and desertion; true, Simon had been reinforced by Llywelwyn's Welsh spearmen, but we have no indication as to their strength. Most writers understandably fight shy of providing an estimate; English Heritage in its *Battlefield Report for Evesham* suggests that there were 10,000 royalists and 5,000 rebels, with some 4,000 of the latter being slain. This is all conjectural but, if we consider that at Lewes the previous year Simon had no more than 500 horse against three times that number, it is most unlikely he had more at Evesham, and he probably had a good deal less. I offer the following suggestion for putative numbers: Simon may have had, say, 300 cavalry, knights and mounted men-at-arms, and no more than, say, 2,500 foot and 1,000 Welsh spears. I would surmise that Edward had, say, 4,000 men in his corps, of whom 500–700 were mounted; I give Mortimer and de Clare each a total strength of 2,500–3,000 men, with perhaps 400–500 being mounted knights. On this basis the royalists enjoyed an overall superiority of three to one, still at least two to one if we accept Mortimer's corps played no actual part in the fight itself (see Appendix 1).

The armies deployed
As the quickening light of a summer's dawn filtered into the

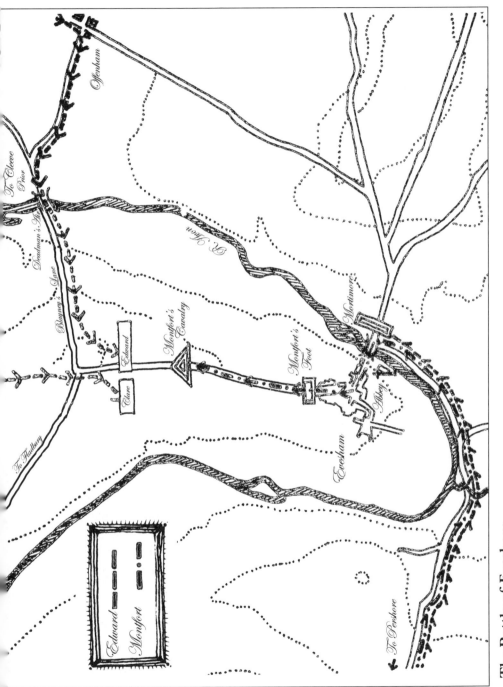

The Battle of Evesham

streets of the market town, these were thronged by a horde of footsore, weary men, amid the collective stench of an army – sweat and unwashed clothing, leather and horse-dung, a raft of bodily odours. They had marched some 15 miles through the hours of darkness over rutted medieval tracks, dried by the sun but layered with thick, clogging dust which would have coated the tired men like a heavy shroud. Removed from the hubbub, king and earl heard mass in the abbey, an extensive Benedictine house; adjacent stood two parish churches, those of All Saints and St Lawrence.

Earl Simon can hardly have consumed his impromptu breakfast when scouts came in to report troop movement to the north. For the present this did not need to augur badly – the earl's barber, known as 'Nicholas of keen eye' and a man familiar with heraldry, reported seeing the banners of the younger Simon and others of the Montfortian faction. He was, of course, deceived: the pennons flaunted were those taken earlier at Kenilworth – the noose was tightening. Still not alarmed – and why should he have been? – Simon gave orders for his division to form up and be prepared to advance. As a safeguard he detailed the sharp-eyed hairdresser to ascend the abbey tower and look out for any sign of the men the earl must have suspected were dogging his march. As he looked out, Nicholas saw the dummy flags droop and the royalist colours raised high; he knew instantly what was occurring and scurried back to report these dire tidings.

Worse, Mortimer's corps was sighted: the back door was sealed off, and only one option other than surrender remained. In this, the moment of absolute crisis, Simon de Montfort did not falter: he knew himself to be out-generalled, outnumbered and without any prospect of retreat – it was fight or die. It is said that, in his bitterness and anger, he blamed the avarice of his sons, but he knew in reality that it was he who commanded and his mistakes, compounded by his own despotic hubris, had brought his affinity to this desperate pass. He accepted that the burden of leadership remained his and his honour would countenance no thought of flight, but he did urge his son Henry, Hugh Despenser and Ralph Basset to attempt escape. To their credit none would abandon the earl, and they prepared to share the hazard of impending battle.

Bishop Cantilupe provided the kneeling knights with absolution, so that they might face death with a clear conscience.[10]

It was now perhaps 8.30 in the morning but, even as the Montfortians hurried to gird themselves for the fight that was now inevitable, the air, which had been heavy and close, suddenly thickened, with darkening skies and an ominous rumble of thunder; lightning flickered over the town, showing the threatening array of hostile colours in stark detail. Rain suddenly lashed down on the men positioned below, the Almighty adding a suitably Wagnerian flourish to what was about to unfold, nature's corollary to man's fury. There may have been some suggestion that the earl should have simply barricaded himself and his men within the abbey precincts and fought a defensive action – this he refused to do, rightly so: sallying out and seeking to break through the ring, whilst a high-risk strategy, at least offered some hope; to become penned like rats in the trap offered none.

We must now consider the line of advance adopted by Simon in leading his army out of the town. Probably the most likely was the route of the present trunk road: for the Montfortians this meant marching due north along High Street, past the last of the houses, across some 300 yards of level ground then the gentle swell of Green Hill.[11] The ascent continued for a further 600 yards toward the line of the ridge; there his enemies awaited. The earl had deployed his forces with the cavalry in column to the front and infantry, under Humphrey de Bohun, behind; the former were of good quality, and the latter, having so many Welsh who were less than enthusiastic, a deal less resolved. Guy de Baliol had the honour of carrying Simon's banner; the king, fully harnessed, rode with the earl, the other men of rank following; with the magnates were many of their household knights – John fitz John, Giles d'Argentan, Fulk of Deane, Harry of Hastings, Peter de Montfort and his two sons Piers and Robert. Each of these men rode with the near-certainty of death, yet none was shown to falter.

It is said that, as they rode out of the abbey gate, Baliol snagged his lance bearing the earl's colours against the lintel, breaking the shaft, an ill omen if one was needed. The town 'lavour' or wash-house probably stood on the northern fringe of the settlement: here Simon halted, presumably to order his knights into a dense marching column, and again offered those who would the chance to flee without dishonour. This could be taken to imply, as Cox would assert, that the bridge was not in fact closed or not closed entirely, and that a means of escape still existed. Here I tend to the view expressed by Tony Spicer that the Montfortians held the bridge, certainly the town end of it, with, quite possibly, a strong guard or picquet on the far side. Mortimer might have been near, even very near, but it is possible that his corps had not fully come up or that the Montfortians were able to hold them off, at least for the interim. De Montfort's urging might be interpreted to imply that the knights, those young men with family responsibilities, should ride clear whilst they could. That he should choose to make these remarks at this particular juncture would suggest he was aware the back door might soon be firmly closed; at present it remained ajar.

Tony Spicer concludes, disagreeing with Cox, that had de Montfort been able to get the whole army away he would have done so; this is entirely sensible – his coming to Evesham in the first place was intended to put distance between himself and Edward. There is no shame in refusing battle against impossible odds; to do otherwise willingly would be at best reckless. De Montfort was not reckless: he fought at Evesham because he had no choice; had he had the means to escape, he would have done so and history would have thought none the worse of him. Nor do I accept that Simon was courting martyrdom: not to fear death is very different from actively seeking to embrace it – quite simply, whatever his failings he, like his father, was a good officer, aware of the heavy burden he carried, with so many men's lives and fortunes hanging on his judgement. He knew he had been humbugged, that no escape route existed; it was his duty then to lead his men clear or fall in the attempt. It was all and the best he could do; Simon de Montfort did not shirk responsibility.

As before, the Montfortians sported their habitual white crosses on right upper arm, front and back.[12] As the demonic heavens rattled above, the dense column of knights made its way up Green Hill, vestiges of settlement giving way to pleasant orchards and fields, heavy with the promise of high summer, the ripe, golden corn standing high. Even with the blackening shroud of the storm whipping about, their proud banners glowed with the richness of the bearer's arms. It was now that Simon recognized de Clare's banner amongst those of his enemies – 'that red dog will devour us today' he is said to have quipped.[13]

Battle joined

If Simon's position was extremely unfavourable, it was not yet completely hopeless. If he could punch through the royalist ring then at least a portion of his force might yet link up with that of the younger Simon, and Evesham might be a reverse rather than a catastrophe. Some chroniclers tell us that the earl formed his men in a circle; this seems unlikely, and a wedge-shaped deployment makes more sense.[14] Green Hill rises no more than 200 feet and we may be confident the main fighting occurred along the ridge-line, though there is some dispute still as to exactly where. If we discount the notion, favoured by some historians, of an attempted flanking movement by the baronial army (see Appendix 1), and follow Rishanger, who asserts that the rebels came straight up the line of the present road (an interpretation followed by Burne and Carpenter), we may thus properly locate the fight where the roads meet – that is, where the east/west axis of High Street meets the north/south line of the Fladbury track (Blayney's Lane). Local tradition records a large number of human bones being found in the land adjoining the old Offenham Bridge – 'Deadman's Ait'.

As the rebels advanced the royalists deployed from marching columns into line – this battle would be the classic duel of line versus column. If we follow Burne and Carpenter, Prince Edward's army formed two wings or battles astride and flanking the Alcester road, directly barring the rebel manoeuvre; Edward on the left, de Clare on the right. We can be reasonably sure that de Montfort was advancing with cavalry in front and infantry behind; we are a good deal less sure of the royalist array – very possibly it was similar, with the mounted arm to the fore and the infantry drawn up behind. Carpenter points out that the prince might have done better to deploy on the lip of the ridge rather than to the rear of the summit on an almost level plateau. When Simon reached the crest his enemies were still some 600 yards distant; nobody was going to be surprised in this encounter. Had the prince had more time then he might well have advanced his banner across that gap, but insufficient time was available.

Here we run into some difficulties with timings. If de Montfort raced from the town at the very first confirmation of a royalist presence then the battle could have begun very early, just after first light. I do not, however, think this altogether likely; for one thing the army had marched all night, and the men would have fallen out to seek rest and sustenance. To get them back in harness, into line, saddled and mounted would have been no easy business. Besides, there was an argument for staying put, delaying any encounter until, hopefully, the younger Simon came up with his power. I tend, therefore, to follow those chroniclers who state the battle was actually fought around the third hour, that is, 7.15–8.30 am.

As the heavens lowered and roared, de Montfort's cavalry dug spurs for the charge, (never likely to be more rapid than a fast canter to maintain cohesion), and his squadrons surged forward over the gently rising ground. Lightning forked as the rebel knights came on, the tattoo of the storm rising around drumming hooves. This was the testing point, when man and beast were poised and welded as one, the lances couched and aimed; the riders stiffened in the saddle, braced for the resounding shock of impact. Not so the rebel foot: once the Welsh levies had seen the proud and overwhelming array of their foes their column disintegrated. The panic as ever proved infectious and the whole force simply dissolved: despite the frenzied curses and ranting of their officers the men could not be brought to rally – de Montfort now had only his mounted arm.

Cox takes the view that the rebels formed a circular ring to withstand the attack, but I disagree. I prefer to think that the Montfortians attacked, as Burne, Carpenter and most other writers assert, and that their initial onslaught made some considerable headway. The charge had gathered weight and the press of mailed horsemen struck deep into the royalist line, attacking at the vulnerable junction between the two divisions. At the *Schwerpunkt* (a phrase borrowed from the German Panzer element of Blitzkrieg – the focus of the attack) Simon enjoyed immediate superiority of numbers; his brigade had the momentum and cohesion of the charge, fuelled by desperation. If he could break through here, the majority of the cavalry could be got off the field; the foot were beyond rally or recall but their loss was not crucial – that of Simon and his mailed horsemen, including some of the leading rebels, would be.

Like breakers pounding on the shore the charge struck home: the Montfortian knights collided with their foes, column versus line, and in that moment it was the column which gained the advantage. Most chroniclers agree that the baronial army drove in the royalists to their front, sheer élan and mass combining into an irresistible momentum. The prince's men were forced back in some confusion; losses were surely incurred, and for a brief, tantalizing moment it seemed that Simon's tactics might prevail and calamity be avoided. Not so; the royalist officers managed to stem the rot, and knights such as Warin of Bassingbourne steadied the shaken rank and file, herding their men back into the fight, probably using the flat of the sword.

Simon failed to create a breakthrough. What he caused was a salient: his charge drove a wedge into the royalist line but did not break through. This was the worst of outcomes, for as the wings of the prince's army swung inwards like revolving doors, the Montfortians became hopelessly entrapped; their partial success proved the basis for their utter destruction. As Carpenter observes, it is quite possible that the fight had moved toward the location of Battle Well (see Appendix 2) and that, as the slaughter unfolded, some were driven along Blayney's Lane and into Deadman's Ait. It would be now that de Montfort formed his survivors into a circle, ready to sell their lives as dearly as possible, for there was no further manoeuvre; that which could be attempted had been tried and had failed. Death was now inevitable, and honour was all that could be salvaged.

And so it was. The Montfortians died hard – Henry, taking station by his father's banner, was said to have led the charge but was overpowered and cut down. More soon fell around him; their horses killed, the rebel knights fought on foot, with sword and mace and axe, their lances blunted or broken. As the blood frenzy seized the prince's and de Clare's men, circling the doomed knights like prowling wolves, one faintly ludicrous figure was that of Henry III of England, the hapless spectator in whose name both sides fought. Henry was no warrior; besides, whom was he to fight? He stood in more danger from a chance blow from his friends than his enemies: despite his harness, he was slightly injured by a lance thrust by one of his son's or the earl's men. His entreaties to all not to lay hands upon their king, plaintive in the circumstances, were finally heeded: Adam de Mohaut recognized the king after removing his helmet. Coming up, Prince Edward took charge of his battered and doubtless bemused parent, and conveyed him to a place of safety; the battle to the death for control of his kingdom continued.[15]

Simon was, for a while, shielded by his household men who fell, like the *huscarls* of old, true to their oaths. Despite the weight of his years and the hopelessness of his position, the earl would think neither of flight nor surrender; whatever his faults, Simon's valour and steadfastness command our respect. As his supporters were hacked down upon the blood-soaked ground, the earl wielded his sword with skill and determination; he accepted death but would not bend his neck as a tamed sacrifice. It is impossible not to feel some empathy with Macbeth when he recovers his dignity in the face of disaster, and so it is with Simon. At length his horse was killed beneath him but still he fought on foot as the ring of his enemies closed about. At least a dozen opponents now assailed the old man, but he would not surrender his sword but with his life. It is said one of the commons struck the earl from behind, sliding a dagger between the rings of his mail. He stumbled and the strength left his limbs as the vengeful blades cut him down. It is said he died well, as we would expect, his last words being 'Dieu, merci' – his tribulations were at an end.[16]

The earl's enemies, in the demonic exhilaration of victory,

stripped the dead man of harness, clothing and dignity; he was, it is said, still wearing a hair shirt. Others went further, including William Maltravers, who savagely and vilely mutilated the corpse, cutting off head, extremities and genitalia. This viciousness was neither ordered nor condoned by the prince, who had sought to save the old man's life, but rather arises from the singular hatred felt by the marchers. Now Cox has Mortimer's men in the fight from the start (see Appendix 1), but I more incline to the view expressed by Tony Spicer. He suggests that the marchers were indeed present but had in fact fought their way over the bridge and then attacked from the rear, following the Montfortians in their route out of the town.[17] This makes excellent sense, and if we accept that, as De Laborderie claims, de Montfort was killed by Mortimer, then there is chronicle evidence, if somewhat tenuous, in support – we do know Simon's severed head was sent to Lady Mortimer at Wigmore, presumably as a gruesome memento.

Aftermath

Ranged around the dreadfully mutilated remains of the dead earl were the corpses of many of his affinity and several leading reformers, including Hugh Despenser, Peter de Montfort, Guy de Baliol, William de Mandeville, Ralph Basset of Drayton, Thomas of Astley, William of Birmingham and Richard Trussel; at least a score of other gentry also fell.[18] Others, such as Harry of Hastings and David of Uffington, were captive: as Cox points out, these last two, amongst 16 men of rank known to have been captured, were taken by marchers, lending some weight to the notion that Mortimer and his affinity were more intensively involved. Of course, de Clare also drew support from the marchers.[19] The younger Simon had led a large mounted contingent from Kenilworth but had halted the column at Alcester so the men might break their fast; as the march was resumed he was greeted by the sight of stumbling fugitives fleeing the stricken field. Stunned and shamed by his tardiness, the survivors turned and rode back to the great fortress where they bottled themselves up behind its great rampart. The younger de Montfort was stricken with guilt over his failure and refused all sustenance for days. His failure had indeed cost his father, brother and their affinity very dear indeed.

An undisclosed number of fleeing men, both on horse and on foot, were hunted down by the whooping victors, their sharp lances spearing men like fish. Some drowned in an attempt to swim the Avon, whilst others were cut down on its banks; some may well have scattered down Blayney's Lane to leave their bones in Deadman's Ait. Yet more sought to hide in gardens or amongst the golden carpet of ripening wheat; their blood soon manured the rich earth. Into the streets and the slaughter continued: men writhed and piled shrieking in the lanes and wynds; some sought sanctuary in the two parochial churches, in the park and cloister, even in the abbey chapel. But there was no sanctuary to be had on that storm-tossed morning, and the whole peninsula was soon carpeted with dead; hacked, mangled and stiffening, blood poured forth in torrents, with a reeking garnish of severed limbs and spilt entrails. With killing came indiscriminate looting, and it would have taken a brave or foolhardy townsman to cling fast to his goods against such a tide. The abbey was not spared and its treasures added wantonly to the victors' haul.[20] So murderous was the assault on the abbey and the desperate survivors sheltering within that the place was regarded as unholy, polluted by the orgy of bloodletting for three decades.[21] A number who escaped Evesham got as far as Tewkesbury, a fief of de Clare, where his adherents made short work of them, littering the streets with yet more carcasses.[22]

Estimates of the total number of dead vary, all probably on the high side, though the fight and pursuit were undoubtedly exceptionally bloody. Cox quotes a figure of 7,500 from the baronial army. I consider this far too high; Carpenter wisely abstains from any assessment, apart from agreeing that the chroniclers' claims are too high, the figure of 10,000 in total being preposterous. My suggestion, and it is no more than that, bearing in mind the projected size of the forces involved, is that the total number of dead was probably between 2,500 and 3,000 at most, the vast majority being from the rebel side. Of Prince Edward's men few of note were slain; Hugh de Troyes and Adam of

Ridware were said to have been killed by their own friends as they had not sported the distinctive red crosses worn by royalists,[23] and Philip of Leominster was another who fell in the melee.

The Battle of Evesham was now over. By midday the baronial army was destroyed and the desperate survivors in hiding or routed; its leaders were dead or captive; Humphrey de Bohun surrendered and joined the train of battered captives herded back to Worcester the day after. For the monks and townsmen the grim business of clearing up began. We sometimes have a view of the medieval period as one of unrelenting bloodshed but this is, of course, quite untrue. Few if any of the inhabitants of Evesham would have witnessed anything other than the occasional local brawl; nothing could have prepared them for this horror. We should not be tempted to glamorize medieval warfare: what was visited on the citizens of the town that day was the equal of the atrocities we have seen within the last decade or so being enacted in the Balkans and elsewhere – brutal, savage, indiscriminate.

On the bloody ground, after the jackals had stripped and scarred the many corpses, lords, gentry and commons were piled in an affinity of the fallen; stench of blood and ordure hung like a shroud in the leaden air. Some of the earl's affinity crept out into the midst of the horror to retrieve their master's remains. How they recognized the shell that was left we cannot say, but the torso was lugged onto a broken ladder for a bier and covered with a tattered cloth – scarcely the pall for a man who had made kings tremble. Simon's remains, together with those of Hugh Despenser and Henry de Montfort, were brought back to the abbey, where the blood of their slaughtered followers gilded the marble. Prince Edward had already given assent so the dead might have decent interment; the king added his consent, so that the fallen lords might be laid under the choir of the abbey church.[24] The prince appeared saddened over the death of his cousin Henry; indeed the savagery on the field seems to have been largely confined to the marchers and their affinity. The earl was not laid to rest till the following day, 5 August, and the monks did the best they could for the rest. The remaining dead were collected under the auspices of the abbey and interred in the existing graveyard, presumably, as Cox suggests, in large pits dug for the purpose.

Simon de Montfort, Earl of Leicester, leader of the reforming faction, was dead, but the constitutional revolution he and others had set in train was not so easily disposed of. The man might have perished, but the legacy would prove rather more enduring.

Chapter 7

Legacy

Greate lester here expir'd with henry his brave sonne
When many a high exploit they, in that day, had donne
Scarce was there noble house of which those times could tell
But that some one thereof, on this or that side, fell.
                              Battle Obelisk, Evesham

Simon de Montfort was dead, and his affinity defeated. With the great earl's demise the baronial cause effectively collapsed, as there was no other magnate of such heroic stature remaining in their shrunken ranks. Evesham was decisive; the war was won even if it was not yet ended. The embers would splutter for many months to come, but what followed was never more than extended mopping-up; the issue was decided by Prince Edward's resounding triumph. Edward's ability to forge an alliance with Mortimer, the marchers and then also de Clare had been critical. We should not overlook the Irish dimension; here the prince had an able champion in Geoffrey de Geneville, who subdued the Montfortians in the province, led by the Geraldines. He accomplished this partly by force of arms and, more tellingly, by skilful diplomacy, giving assurances on land tenure and procuring the release of the captured royal official Richard de la Rochelle.[1]

The royalist triumph
Though Simon the Younger had been diminished and chastened by the raid on Kenilworth, his substantial forces remained in the

field, together with a crop of Montfortian garrisons and diehards across the breadth of the realm. Evesham marked Prince Edward's true coming of age. Unlike the previous campaign of Lewes, Henry III had played no active part; the mopping-up was also undertaken by Longshanks. With the vigour that so characterized his future military career Edward did not linger on the field. After Evesham he marched north into his own lands of Chester; his authority here required robust assertion. From Chester two officers, Roger Leyburn and Nicholas de Lewknor, the latter keeper of the wardrobe, were detailed to ensure de Warenne was suitably resourced to subdue the Cinque Ports and re-establish the royal writ in Kent. Those defenders still holding out behind Kenilworth's massive ramparts and in other castles such as Wallingford and Berkhamsted were summoned to surrender; the terms offered were moderate, in the circumstances. Edward was understandably anxious to be done with the business of rebellion.

Moderation was not necessarily a feature of royalist policy overall. The September Parliament was to summon the wives or widows of those rebels taken or slain; all faced attainder. Parliament appointed commissioners whose role was to assist the sheriffs in enforcing the seizures. The defeat and death of de Montfort did not deter his ally Llywelwyn, who energetically took up parts of Cheshire; a royal riposte headed by Hamo Lestrange and Maurice FitzGerald received a sound drubbing from the Welsh. The king had moved to Windsor via Winchester where, recovering from his humiliation at the hands of the Montfortians and the hurts he had had in battle, Henry prepared to settle his account with turbulent London. The burgesses were much alarmed, and with good cause; the mayor and two-score leading citizens came out, relying on safe conducts negotiated with Roger Leyburn, but the king was minded to teach these contumacious subjects a lesson. They were summarily arrested, with the mayor and a handful of others handed over to Edward's custody.

The prince, as we will recall, had a particular grievance against the Londoners for the imprudent abuse they had offered his mother, the queen; a number of forfeited properties were redistributed amongst the prince's affinity.[2] Such intemperance was about to cost the Londoners dear. Drafts of letters which would have offered amnesty were held back and no firm undertakings issued until early December; the official pardon was not granted until January 1266. In the interim, the king, having regained his capital, ensured his wayward citizens paid handsomely for their mistakes; even the final amnesty was only issued on payment of a general fine of 20,000 marks.[3]

By the end of October, the Londoners having been chastised, Edward was marching on Dover, where Eleanor de Montfort surrendered the castle; resistance if any was muted, and the garrison departed on terms. He was also able to welcome his formidable mother, who arrived with the papal legate. Simon the Younger had withdrawn the rump of his forces, together with diehards Baldwin Wake and John d'Eyville; they took refuge in the wild, watery recesses of the fens in north Lincolnshire, concentrated on the Isle of Axholme. Edward, as ever, displayed energy together with sound tactical sense; having gathered shire levies from Nottinghamshire and Derbyshire, he threw pontoon bridges across the wetlands and compelled the rebels to terms by Christmas. Those terms offered were, in the circumstances, generous, and though Simon, true to his undertaking, did appear before Parliament, he disappeared before any sentence could be passed. Both Wake and d'Eyville were tardy in cementing their peace.

Having dealt with Simon, Edward hurried back to the south coast, where the Cinque Ports burgesses were proving obstinate: these proved a rather tougher nut than the rebels skulking in the Lincolnshire marches, and were not subdued until Winchelsea fell to amphibious assault. A final surrender was not concluded until 30 May 1266; again the terms were generous. The prince's continued run of successes garnered several significant plums, the governorship of Dover and stewardship of the Cinque Ports being but two. Kent was now secure, but further campaigning was still required; Leyburn advanced into Essex, whilst the prince moved on the remaining rebels in Hampshire. It was here that an incident, the stuff of chivalric legend, occurred. In the Forest of

Alton, in what may have been a confused skirmish, the rebel
knight Adam Gurdon, a leading local Montfortian, and Edward
clashed in single combat. Gurdon was a doughty fighter with
something of a reputation, and the encounter assumed the
proportions of a Homeric duel, long and hard-fought but with
honour on both sides. The prince bested his opponent, whose
partisans also came off rather worse, with several men lost in the
fight and others dancing at ropes' end. Edward was prepared to
show mercy to a worthy adversary and spared Gurdon, who found
himself incarcerated at Windsor; he was in elevated company, for
the Earl of Derby, who had been taken by Henry of Almain at
Chesterfield, was also an inmate.[4]

The siege of Kenilworth

All of these mini-campaigns were signal successes and the various
rebel enclaves were mopped up without serious loss; Kenilworth,
however, still remained defiant, and the subsequent leaguer was to
be a true epic on the scale of Rochester in the earlier war. The
castle, as we have noted, came to de Montfort in 1244, and he had
greatly   strengthened   an   already   formidable   enceinte.
Commanding a rocky knoll which swells imposingly from
surrounding wetlands, the red sandstone fortress dominates the
surrounding plain. King John had originally replaced the timber
motte thrown up by Geoffrey de Clinton with a stone donjon,
adding an outer bailey; it was John who also built the strengthened
dam or causeway. To the west and south the approach was covered
by an expanse of water, the Mere, some 20 hectares in breadth.
The outer bailey wall was lengthy, enclosing a substantial area and
studded with projecting towers. The inner ward was far stronger,
dominated by lofty square towers and the imposing keep. The
system of water obstacles meant the fortress was virtually an
island; to the wide sweep of the Mere was added a broad moat on
the northern flank which lapped around as far as the Lower Pool,
a further square-shaped miniature lake. This shielded the
causeway which ran north-westwards from the fortified outwork
on the Brays. This was, in turn, again girded by water. The whole
constituted a besieger's nightmare, and at the time of the siege was

strongly garrisoned by some 1,200 determined and desperate defenders.

Prince Edward was not initially involved in the siege operations, these being entrusted to his younger brother Edmund. It was to prove a vast undertaking, and Prince Edmund had mobilized levies from ten counties. These laboured to provide timber for great engines of war, built to hammer the walls; monster trebuchets set up in the south-west quadrant battered away at the Brays, whilst others ringed the north and east. The siege, though long and equally arduous for both defenders and besiegers, was not without incident. Those within kept up a cheering barrage of abuse, whilst the royalists sought to overcome the obstacle of the Mere by amphibious escalade, drawing landing craft down from Chester – a very costly and ultimately futile endeavour. As the military solution appeared distant, a committee of twelve was established in late August 1266. Prince Edward was not a member of this panel, nor were his interests strongly represented;[5] there may have been policy in this, as Edward's attitude to the rebels was perhaps perceived as both harsh and mercenary. Henry of Almain and the papal legate were the appointed arbitrators, and by 31 October they had drafted the Dictum of Kenilworth. The key provision was that those attainted might buy back their confiscated estates, with prices fixed on a sliding tariff dependent upon the level of culpability. For those most implicated, including the Kenilworth garrison, this was a rather feeble inducement and did not immediately bring the prolonged leaguer to an end. Hunger finally opened the gates in December, the garrison starved and reeking.[6]

Kenilworth's fall was an important step toward a conclusion of hostilities but disturbances were not yet at an end. In distant Northumberland, John de Vesci, one of those taken at Evesham and further disaffected by draconian sequestrations, rebelled.[7] Edward was obliged to quit the siege lines and hurry north to confront de Vesci, who bent his knee at Alnwick, and incurred a swingeing fine of 3,700 marks.[8] Whilst in the wild north the prince recruited some additional Scottish borderers as mercenaries before marching south to deal with John d'Eyeville, skulking on

Ely, and quasi-guerrilla warfare spluttered on over the winter. The Parliament summoned to Bury St Edmunds in February accomplished little, and further amphibious operations proved abortive. D'Eyeville's continued defiance, of itself, was more nuisance than threat, but the situation was once again transformed in April 1267 when Gilbert de Clare, Earl of Gloucester, decided, once again, to swap sides and plant his defiant banners firmly in the streets of the capital. De Clare had a string of grievances, mostly centred on frustrated self-interest – he was at loggerheads with Mortimer over the control of Humphrey de Bohun's marcher holdings and at odds with the crown over dower lands occupied by his mother, and may generally have felt the rewards he had received were not commensurate with his vital contribution. More altruistically, he was deeply unhappy over the severity of treatment meted out to the defeated rebels.

The end of the war
For a tense moment, the situation appeared serious; John d'Eyville had joined the earl in London and the burgesses, still smarting from their earlier treatment, were vociferous in their support. To lay siege to London was virtually inconceivable; Kenilworth's leaguer had gobbled up a vast amount of treasure. One of those caught up in these fresh alarums was the papal legate lodged in the Tower, and it was his calls for moderation, backed by others who had no desire to witness a resumption of civil strife, which prevailed. De Clare was persuaded to negotiate; Richard of Cornwall, Henry of Almain and Philip Basset acted as brokers; and the earl laid down arms, quit the capital and stumped up a hefty security.

This affair was not without consequence, nor was the earl's protest in vain. From this point on, June 1267, the royalists seemed to draw breath and understand that peace could not be guaranteed by the edge of the sword, and that some measure of fair play was required. As an indication of this more conciliatory climate d'Eyeville, Nicholas Seagrave, Norman d'Arcy and the rump of the remaining diehards came in and sought the king's peace – they were not refused. A few still held out on Ely, but with the marshes drying in the summer heat and a clear warning having been issued to those who remained under arms, Edward secured their final surrender. The war was, at long last, over.

It was now time to deal with the Welsh and, on 29 September, Llywelwyn agreed terms; the Treaty of Montgomery brought the alarums along the frontier to a temporary end. The Welshman was confirmed in his titles, a local magnate to whom the lesser Welsh lords owed homage, as did the prince himself to Henry III; the disputed lands of the four Cantreds were formally assigned to Llywelwyn. In November the Statute of Marlborough was enacted, which, in many ways, echoed the process of reform begun in 1259.

What, then, besides loss of life, despoliation, pain and loss had the Second Barons' War achieved? Outwardly little, for the king's power appeared untouched and the baronial opposition were either dead or cowed, their armies destroyed and their castles taken. Yet it was not all for nothing: the legend of de Montfort lived on and he is popularly regarded as the father of the English parliamentary system. It is true he failed to secure the lasting effect of the Provisions of Oxford, and he certainly did not succeed in his ambition to found a great and lasting dynasty at the heart of the English polity. Yet, for all that, his nobler qualities endure: the ageing paladin who led his army up that desperate slope at Evesham rode proudly to near-certain death not just for glory or for greed but for an ideal, a concept of government and statehood that lives on with us today. If that is not quite greatness then it is something very like.

The last blow had not yet been struck – de Montfort's sons Simon and Guy pursued their erratic and violent careers in the service of France. In 1268 both fought in Italy for Charles of Anjou, a campaign which ended with the conquest of Sicily, and rose in his service. Their advancement was fatally marred by a crime they jointly committed on 13 March 1271: Henry of Almain, whilst at prayer in Viterbo, was attacked and savagely done to death. Guy it was who bore the knife, abetted by his brother. As the stricken Henry begged for mercy, he received the unrelenting response, 'You had no mercy on my father and brothers . . . I have taken my vengeance."[9] Simon, hunted and reviled for the murder, died in obscurity the very same year; Guy survived for another two decades before expiring in a Sicilian gaol, around 1291. The de Montfort dynasty did not, as the elder Simon had hoped, become one of the great houses of the English polity but died out in penurious disgrace, shunned and despised.

Appendix 1

Evesham:
An Alternative View

There is yet some disagreement as to the detail of the fight and the approach of the royal army. Oman's view, as described above, was that Edward divided the army into three brigades, whilst still at Worcester. That commanded by Mortimer effectively dogged the footsteps of de Montfort's army; the second, under de Clare, advanced via the Worcester Road–Evesham Road (A44), which steers north of the Avon to attain Green Hill, roughly a mile north of the town. The prince traversed the line of the present A422 by Inkberrow, over what is now the B4088, moving south to also reach Green Hill. In this Sir Charles draws heavily on Guisborough and Trevet. The subsequent objectors point out, with good reason, the difficulties involved in marching in three divisions, and that a capable general, which Edward most assuredly was, would refrain from splitting his command until the last moment. Part of the weight of Oman's argument rests on the identification of 'Clive' in Trevet with Cleeve Prior.

Ramsay argues that the prince crossed the Avon at Cleeve Prior and marched along the eastern flank to Offenham, where he detailed Mortimer to block the bridge leading from Evesham before leading his two remaining brigades back over the Avon at Offenham to approach Green Hill. This theory is then expanded to locate the main fighting by the position of the Victorian obelisk.

Simon was attempting to get his forces to the Green Hill crossroads before the royalists but was herded west by the weight of numbers pouring up to Blayney's Lane. Cox, however, takes an altogether different line – rejecting the notion that the royalists crossed at Cleeve Prior, he quite simply avers that the royal army advanced united and deployed in three divisions on Green Hill. He uses as evidence the fact that none of the chroniclers mentions Mortimer blocking the bridge at Evesham or a second crossing of the Avon at Offenham.

Core to Cox's argument is the identification of Clive not as Cleeve Prior but as Clevelode, where de Montfort crossed the Severn on 2 August; to follow Cox we must also be prepared to dismiss Guisborough and Evesham, both accepted sources. For Carpenter this is a leap of faith too far and he rejects Cox's theory: even though he recognizes its seductive qualities, he feels that Guisborough's account of Mortimer's deployment – that he came toward the Montfortians around the abbey from the west rear – is compelling and consistent. The flaw in Cox's argument is that the deployment he favours would have left the bridge unguarded, and thus the 'back door' would have been open as an escape route. He cites the insistence, agreed by several sources, that de Montfort disdained to fly. Such defiance would be typical of the earl's uncompromising nature and yet, as Carpenter observes, for de Montfort to draw off his forces intact in the face of such odds and unfavourable ground would have entailed no shame; had this course been open to him then it seems certain he would have acted accordingly. Carpenter likewise rejects Cox's assertion that de Montfort fell at the location named 'God's Croft' – possibly identified with a nineteenth-century property some 300 yards south of Green Hill.

Local historian Tony Spicer has put forward yet another view. He, like Cox, draws on the fourteenth-century chronicle set out in *EHR*.[1] This source suggests the de Montfortians considered defending the abbey precincts but that the earl preferred to fight in the open; as the army debouched from the town and reached the 'lavour' (civic washhouse) he then offered those who sought safety to flee across the bridge. The source avers the royalists came on in three divisions and that Simon himself died by the hand of Roger Mortimer. A key assertion is that before the fight Edward and de Clare were together in Mosham Meadow – this is believed to have lain between the banks of the Avon and the Worcester road, below Craycombe Hill, thus supporting the contention the prince's army had simply advanced directly from Worcester as a united command. The suggestion that Simon was able to offer a chance of flight to the more faint-hearted is cited as evidence the bridge was not sealed off. Spicer suggests the Montfortians thus still held the bridge with a sufficient guard to guarantee a viable escape route. This assumes Mortimer had not fully come up and had made no serious attempt to storm or blockade the bridge.

Spicer goes on to argue that for Mortimer to have been credited with striking down the earl – and there was a very high degree of animosity: chroniclers concur that the body parts barbarously hacked from the corpse were sent as grisly trophies to Lady Mortimer – then he must have taken part in the fighting and been south of the Avon. Spicer goes on to assert that Mortimer's brigade had not been involved in the raid on Kenilworth; he remained at Worcester, with all his power, to block any attempt by the earl to attempt the dash from Kempsey and link up with his son. Assuming that some outpost bickering did occur, then it is not illogical to see Mortimer dogging the earl's march to Evesham. The marcher lord was a seasoned campaigner used to exercising a fair degree of initiative, his personal hatreds acting as an additional spur to continued action. De Montfort crossed the bridge to put his troops into Evesham and also to place the river barrier between his forces and a pursuer, the bridge itself being relatively easy to defend.

Once alerted to his imminent peril, de Montfort attempted to break out to the west and slip past the royalist forces deploying on Green Hill. He kept the foot on the right, next to the Avon, with the horse on the left; he left a commanded party to hold the bridge in rear. Edward had foreseen this and de Clare's brigade was already moving north-eastwards from Mosham Meadow, his progress hidden from de Montfort by intervening dead ground (this may be the ground referred to in Chapter 6, note 9). Spicer thus places the initial clash at or near Siveldeston with the Welsh foot bearing the brunt; these did not stand but broke and fled, with some attempting to reach the narrow bridge at Offenham; Deadman's Ait is so named from the slaughter which ensued there. De Montfort kept his cavalry in hand but de Clare's men were pressing hard. He espied a possible gap in the thickening royalist line toward Green Hill. He swung his column around and they now crashed into the unprepared flank of the prince's brigade, their advance taking them along Blayney's Lane, ascending Green Hill by the eastern approach.

This attack, though dangerous, the combat of line over column, did not result in a breakthrough; de Montfort's charge was held, even if the royalists gave ground. With momentum lost, the baronial army was increasingly overwhelmed by superior numbers. Spicer's theory allows for Mortimer to deliver the *coup de grâce*: he suggested the marchers fight their way over the bridge at Bengeworth and fall upon the remains of the baronial army from the rear – thus it was Mortimer or men of his affinity who cut down the earl and those about him. This theory is rather attractive: if we stray from strict reliance on the chronicle accounts where the latter are unclear and into the realm of what Burne would have described as 'inherent military probability', the argument contains some compelling elements.

I agree with Spicer (who follows Ramsay here) in his assessment of the situation at Worcester and his interpretation of the attack on Kenilworth, for the reasons previously set out. I find his idea of Mortimer's independent action attractive though, of course, unproven; that he should shadow de Montfort after successfully maintaining a blocking position at Worcester is feasible, that his brigade should follow the baronial army to Evesham is likewise possible; that he should attack the bridge defenders when the main Montfortian force was committed to its breakout attempt is also entirely credible.[2] I also find the idea that de Montfort selected a westerly line of march from Evesham questionable, as both Westminster[3] and Rishanger are quite specific in asserting the baronial army moved straight up the slope toward Green Hill; Burne and Carpenter both discount the notion of a flanking march on the basis of an assessment of the ground and the difficulties which crossing a defile and making a steep ascent would have entailed. In this I think they are quite right.

Appendix 2

The Battlefield Trail

Lewes: OS grid reference TQ399111 (539988 111128); OS Landranger map 198, Explorer map 122
The town of Lewes has now, inconveniently for the battlefield detective, spilled outwards from its Saxon and medieval core, now extending significantly north and west of the castle and priory site. By the mid-thirteenth century it was an established and bustling market town and port, retaining the classic Saxon pattern of a principal thoroughfare (High Street) with lanes running off laterally. Both the priory and St Anne's church stood at the time. The settlement, with some fourteen churches, a merchant guild and a market, prospered on the backs of fat sheep driven in from the Downs and beasts, leather and iron ore from the Weald, and the harbour took delivery of wines from Bordeaux. Meadowland flooded below the swell of the Downs but the area has perhaps not changed overmuch in terms of land usage; more ground is now under the plough and the eighteenth-century racecourse behind the line once held by the baronial army's right-hand division.

Suburban sprawl now obscures the line of Prince Edward's advance and the later fighting around the outskirts. However, Simon's position on the plateau of Offham Hill may be attained by following the path from just opposite Offham church on the present A275, some two miles (3km) north of Lewes. As you ascend, the chalk pits will be on your left. Having crossed a stile you then turn right toward a small reservoir. Here you are overlooking the town and the falling ground to Landport Bottom. You are now standing where the left wing of the baronial army, the Londoners, took station, and from where they were routed by Prince Edward's knights. If you look to your right you can plainly discern where the front line of de Montfort's divisions would have been on the day of the battle; to your right rear is the ground taken by the reserve. A further monument stands on Harry's Hill to your right rear, which can be reached by a footpath.

Lewes Castle survives. Built by William de Warenne in around 1069–1070, it became the family's main seat after he was raised to the earldom of Surrey in 1088. The shell keep (early twelfth century) and its later semi-octagonal towers were part of the enceinte in 1264; the superb barbican is a later addition, dating from the fourteenth century. The visitor may walk from the castle, down St Martin's Lane, into Garden Street and then onto Priory Road; little of the significant Cluniac house, the first in England, remains. Beside the children's playground, a rather unlikely setting, stands the present battlefield memorial, designed by Enzo Plazotta in 1964 for the 700th anniversary, and presented to the town by the then MP Sir Tufton Beamish (later Lord Chelwood). This is fashioned as a representation of a great helm with an inscribed circlet on which is written:

> Law is like fire for it lights the truth, warms as charity, burns as zeal. With these virtues the King will rule well. Now Englishmen read on about this battle fought at Lewes' Walls because of this you are alive and safe, rejoice then in God.

Some traces of the old town walls survive in Southover Road and there is sufficient sense of the old town to afford an idea of the scale and general layout at the time of the battle. Rochester Castle too survives; the great keep was originally raised in the twelfth century by William le Corbeil, Archbishop of Canterbury, who had received a grant of the place from Henry I. Despite the sieges and vicissitudes since, the massive donjon, some 34.5m high, remains the tallest in England. Henry III carried out extensive rebuilding after the epic siege conducted by his father. Both

Longshanks and then Edward III undertook further building. A fortified tower, the water bastion, overlooked the original medieval bridge, which stood some distance upstream from its successor.

A series of what may be graves were uncovered in the Offham chalk pits. Some caution must be exercised as the fact that the dead were interred in small excavations with six to nine bodies apiece raises the possibility these dead were later victims of pestilence rather than war. It might, however, be that many of those Londoners cut down in the exultant fury of Prince Edward's charge were deposited here. In 1810, whilst work was being carried out at the town gaol, three mass burials, each holding half a thousand, were revealed; such a concentration clearly points to battlefield casualties. Over three and a half decades later a further mass interment was uncovered in the grounds of the former priory in the course of railway engineering works. The bones were found in what may have been a well some 18ft (5m) below ground level. Ten wagonloads were subsequently removed and, in the modern idiom, immediately 'recycled' as fill for an embankment at Southerham, then under construction. As the *Sussex Express* leader of 17 January 1846 lamented: 'It is a source of deep regret that human bones should have been employed for such a purpose.' A local doctor, Gideon Mansell, further expounded:

> In perfect accordance with the spirit of this railway age, this heap of skeletons of the patriots and royalists of the thirteenth century, which filled thirteen wagons [three more than the newspaper report], was taken away to form part of the embankment of the line in the adjacent brook.

Evesham: OS grid reference SP039455 (403950 245530); OS Landranger map 150; Explorer map 205
There is little disagreement about the location of the battlefield. Edward's army on the morning of the battle ascended Green Hill, a mile or so north of the town, most likely in the vicinity of 'Siveldeston', named after the ancient Saxon marker 'Siflaed's

Stone'. This was erected on the 'salt street' (now followed by Blayney's Lane), which fixed either the northern boundary of the settlement or the flank of the abbatial holdings. The antiquary William Tindal viewed the stone in the eighteenth century, though it was removed before he died in 1804. It was commonly believed to commemorate the site of the battle, though this is incorrect, as its erection pre-dates the fight by several centuries. 'Battle Well', more realistically considered to be the spot where Simon breathed his last, became the focus for a cult of veneration and a regular destination for pilgrims prior to the Reformation. The spring itself was not discovered until the year following the battle by Piers of Saltmarsh. An account written in the mid-fifteenth century by a monk from St Albans records a stand of elms about the well with a crude stone shrine. The more cynical might suspect the monks of Evesham of spotting a lucrative opportunity.

Much of the land above the town was enclosed following the 1827 Enclosure Act. The buildings formed a ribbon settlement flowing from the abbey precincts, with only the bridge at Bengeworth offering a single crossing over the deep loop of the Avon. It is likely the present A435 picks up the line of the medieval road that led north, rising to Green Hill. Despite any hard evidence it may be supposed that the ground was covered by open fields, though the higher ground was more likely bare, rough grazing and moor. The inevitable spread of the town and its suburbs, together with the enclosure and more intensive farming of the open ground, has considerably distorted the picture of the area as it would have appeared to the protagonists of 1265.

Evesham, for such an important field, has little to excite the visitor today, as most of the combat occurred over ground which is now in private ownership and heavily cultivated. Much good work is presently being undertaken by the Simon de Montfort Society to improve access and provide interpretation (www.simondemontfort.org). The site of Battle Well lies some 65 yards (59m) south of the B4084 and approximately 40 yards (37m) west of the present A435; access is difficult and the site no more than a rather ill-defined depression. The town inevitably has expanded very considerably, though its location in the significant loop of the River Avon has not. A perambulation beginning at the abbey garden entrance will, after a right-hand turn, bring you to the memorial, formed from stone from the de Montforts' seat in France, unveiled by the Archbishop of Canterbury in 1965. It was from the tower of the abbey church that Simon's barber is said to have spotted the royalist approach; there is a good range of interpretation panels indicating the appearance and extent of the abbey. The town's museum, the delightful Almonry, has a dedicated de Montfort display.

To follow the route taken by the baronial army you simply need to follow the line of the present High Street and then the Alcester road; obviously the present spread of development greatly surpasses the much more modest township of the thirteenth century. As you reach the brow of the hill, across from Croft Road is Battle Well House (not to be confused with the Battle Well as such) – it is here that evidence of burial pits was discovered in the nineteenth century. As you continue in a northerly direction and before you reach Blayney's Lane (to the right) there is a footpath (private) leading to the spot where, as it is believed, the earl met his death. As you proceed, look for the left turning onto the Squires which leads you along the line held by Gloucester's division, with Prince Edward's command deployed east of the junction and on your right. The Y junction you have just passed may mark the very point of contact, where the baronial column crashed into the royalist line. You now stand on ground where the history of England was decided.

Previously access to the obelisk was restricted as it stands within the grounds of Abbey Manor House, private property; more recently a footpath has been provided (with the aid of the Forestry Commission grants scheme) and this leads from a car park on the Squires to the Leicester Tower and then to the obelisk. Its inscription reads:

ON THIS SPOT IN THE REIGN OF HENRY III THE BATTLE OF EVESHAM WAS FOUGHT, AUGUST 4TH 1265, BETWEEN THE KING'S FORCES COMMANDED BY HIS ELDEST SON PRINCE

EDWARD AND THE BARONS UNDER SIMON DE MONTFORT
EARL OF LEICESTER; IN WHICH THE PRINCE BY HIS SKILL AND
VALOUR OBTAINED A COMPLETE VICTORY AND THE EARL
AND HIS ELDEST SON HENRY DE MONTFORT, 18 BARONS, 160
KNIGHTS, AND 4,000 SOLDIERS, WERE SLAIN IN THE BATTLE.

It was the strength of local faith that the Battle Well site marked the epicentre of the fight, argued by nineteenth-century local antiquarian E.J. Rudge, that persuaded the owner of the regency manor (Rudge's father) to erect the obelisk in 1821. On the Pershore road a short distance from Evesham stands Flatbury church. It is said the stained glass in the north chancel window, bearing Simon's arms and restored at the same time that the modern memorial was erected, was rescued from the wrack of the abbey during the dissolution.

Perhaps the most impressive survivor of the campaign of 1265 is Kenilworth Castle itself. The remains, which today are in the care of English Heritage, still convey the scale and majesty of the place, rising from marshland in a great red sandstone mass upon its hillock. The motte was probably thrown up in the opening decades of the twelfth century by Geoffrey de Clinton, but the main building was undertaken by John after the place had reverted to the crown. It was he who built the outer curtain and created the initial water defences; the wide expanse of the Mere created a large artificial lake to the west and south. It was in 1244 that the castle came into Simon de Montfort's possession. It continued to resist even after the disaster at Evesham, and defied the besiegers' best efforts for half a year. This was by no means the conclusion of its active history: it passed through the earls and, latterly, dukes of Lancaster to John of Gaunt and, in the sixteenth century, to Robert Dudley, earl of Leicester, Elizabeth I's favourite and possible lover. Much of what survives dates from later building, but the great keep and some of the enceinte gives a fine impression of its great strength in the thirteenth century. An exhibition mounted by EH features representations of the castle during its various phases.

Appendix 3

Wargaming the Battles of Lewes and Evesham

For those who play board games, Clash of Arms Games produces the excellent *Barons' War – the Battles of Lewes and Evesham*, which focuses upon the two campaigns. Each map hex is approximately 100 yards from side to side, with each infantry strength representing 50–75 men and the cavalry strength points representing 30–45 men. Board games have the dual advantages of being inexpensive and quick to set up. For those anxious to replay the two key fights of the Barons' War the game is ideal.

Terrain: at Lewes the action should be bounded by the castle and priory occupying the south-easterly quadrant of the board, with the river delineating the eastern boundary and the summit of the Downs forming the baronial start line. For Evesham the table should be bounded on the east, south and west by the Avon (unfordable). If Mortimer's forces remain inert, simply blocking, then there is little need to bring them on; we simply assume that the baronial forces must break out to the north or perish in the attempt. A question arises as to whether the gamer needs to consider the rising contours – clearly this is highly relevant, as the baronial player must decide if they intend to strike straight up the road or attempt to manoeuvre by the left flank.

When setting up war games for this period I tend to prefer 25mm figures – I consider they possess more individual character and can be used for skirmishing; attending to detail on surcoats and liveries is easier, than with, say, 15mm figures. Many companies now produce good ranges of figures for the period, Foundry, Front Rank and Old Glory being good examples. Most gamers tend to modify the standard roles to suit and I'm thoroughly in accord with this. In terms of rules both DBM and DBA are useful as is 'Day of Battle' or, better still, 'Flower of Chivalry' and perhaps 'Warhammer Ancient Battles'.

Considering figure ratios I would suggest 1:50; 25mm figures are ideal for skirmishing particular elements of the action. With Lewes, an interesting variant would be allowing Prince Edward to rally and redeploy rather faster than occurred, thus bringing his forces back onto the field at the crisis point. At Evesham the objectives of the players are straightforward: de Montfort is seeking to break out of the ring and Prince Edward seeks to prevent this. A number of variations can be introduced – such as permitting Mortimer to launch an attack on the bridge, force a passage and thereupon fall on the rear of the beleaguered baronial army. It would also be possible to introduce the younger de Montfort's forces onto the table; their arrival in time could, of course, significantly affect the outcome.

Glossary

Arming cap	a padded fabric hood, worn under a metal helmet
Ballista	a form of catapult, dating from the classical era, shooting a missile from an integral bow, tensioned by the operation of a windlass
Banneret	a military rank, the holder thereof rated above a knight and entitled to a square banner, rather than a knightly **pennon**
Barbican	an outwork constructed so as to provide protection for a castle or the fortified gateway of a town; it could be erected in stone, thus permanent, or in timber as a temporary additional defence
Battle (Battail)	a division or corps of an army
Belfry	a wooden siege tower, moved forward against the enemy's walls on wheels or rollers
Bill	a polearm, born of the union of the agricultural tool with the military spear to create a formidable hafted weapon
Blazon	the formal description of a coat of arms or banner
Bolt	a short, thick arrow or quarrel, shot from a crossbow
Bracer	a section of plate defence for the lower arm
Brattice	a form of timber hoarding built onto the parapet of a castle and corbelled out on wooden beams, providing a protected shooting gallery for the defenders' bows

Brigandine	a protective, flexible doublet with horn or metal plates sewn in
Broadsword	a double-edged, generally single-handed knightly sword
Buckler	a small round shield or target used for parrying an opponent's weapon and delivering fast beats or punches
Caparison	a fabric horse-covering intended both for decoration and for defence, usually padded accordingly
Captain	the officer in charge of a particular location, whose authority was limited to that place and did not extend beyond
Chamfron	a section of plate armour covering a horse's head
Chausee	stockings of mail intended to afford protection to the horseman's calves
Chevauchee	a large spoiling raid into enemy territory, a form of economic warfare
Coif	a mail hood worn under the helmet but over the arming cap
Conroi	a mounted detachment
Crenellation	the castle battlements along the parapet walk – licence to crenellate being, in effect, the requisite planning permission to construct a castle; in times of strife, such as the wars between Stephen and Matilda, many rogue castles were thrown up by warring lords
Destrier	the knightly warhorse
Enceinte	the circuit of a defensible place
Escalade	an assault aimed at storming defences
Falchion	a broad-bladed, cleaver-like weapon
Fief	the feudal landholding
Fuller	the central groove or grooves running down a sword blade, to assist balance and weight
Harness	a full armour of plate, mail or both combined

Hauberk	a mail shirt, reaching to the knee, the habergeon being the shorter version
Helm	the thirteenth-century great helmet worn by knights
Hide	a measure of land, not consistent but generally equal to 120 acres
Jack	a utility form of **brigandine**, the garment stuffed with rags or tallow
Leaguer	a siege or blockade
Mangonel	an engine for throwing stones – again of classical provenance
Melee	contact between large forces, either mounted or on foot
Mesnie	a household knight, of the lord's estate or 'demesne'
Motte and Bailey	a form of Norman timber castle, with a raised lower ward containing the normal domestic range, protected by ditch and palisade and with a higher conical mound surmounted by a timber tower, the final refuge for the garrison when assailed
Palfrey	an everyday horse
Pennon (or pennant)	one of the principal types of medieval flags (from the Latin 'penna', i.e. 'wing' or 'feather')
Pricker	a scout or skirmisher
Quillons	the crossbars at the base of the sword hilt which afford the holder protection
Surcoat	a long, flowing fabric garment worn over harness carrying the arms or **blazon** of the knight
Trapper	padded horse protection
Trebuchet	a large siege engine with a heavy throwing arm

Notes

Chapter 1. Background: Of Arms and Men

1. Homer, *The Iliad*, book XII, trans. W.H.D. Rouse (London, 1964).
2. Burne, Colonel A., *The Battlefields of England* (London, 1951), p. 53.
3. Norman, A.V.B., and D. Pottinger, *English Weapons and Warfare, 449–1660* (London, 1966), p. 60.
4. Feudal homage was the due owed by vassal to lord, the extent of which might vary according to the terms of the oath which had been sworn, but might extend to full military obligation.
5. Prestwich, M., *Armies and Warfare in the Middle Ages* (London, 1966), p. 58.
6. During the Falkirk campaign, supplies had run low and the men had become discontented; a shipment of wine from the fleet was poured into empty bellies and a fracas arose between the English and Welsh.
7. Jean le Bel reported the brawl between the English and Hainaulters prior to the Weardale campaign; many heads were broken in consequence. See Prestwich, op. cit., p. 178.
8. The bishop was perceived as a particular intimate of King John and was widely disliked.
9. Oman, Sir C., *The Art of War in the Middle Ages*, vol. 1 (London, 1924), p. 418.
10. Prestwich, op. cit., p. 178.
11. Boardman, A., *The Medieval Soldier in the Wars of the Roses* (London, 1998), p. 173.
12. Traquair, P., *Freedom's Sword* (London, 1998), p. 289.

13. Writer and explorer Tim Severin, as Professor Prestwich points out, attempted to identify the closest modern mount to the medieval destrier: he favoured a heavy horse from the Ardennes, powerful and resilient but rather too broad in the back for continuous days in the saddle. Knights were relatively few at this time, perhaps no more than 1,250 in all in England. See Denholm-Young, N., 'Feudal Society in the Thirteenth Century: The Knights', in *Collected Papers* (Cardiff, 1969).

14. Prestwich, op. cit., pp. 1–2.

15. Gravett, C., *Medieval Siege Warfare* (England, 1990), p. 50.

16. Arnaud Amaury was the papal legate in a campaign that was largely influenced by the genius of Simon de Montfort's remarkable father, the elder Simon.

17. *Bouches inutiles*, literally 'useless mouths' – those who were of no military value in the defence.

18. A fireship was an expedient derived from classical times, a redundant vessel crammed with combustibles and fired as it approached the enemy ships or installation; the skeleton crew then abandoned ship. Used properly against timber structures they could be devastating.

19. Henry III subsequently refurbished Rochester, adding to and rebuilding the chapel and domestic offices. He also restored the damaged south-east tower, but this was rebuilt as three-quarter round, whilst the earlier surviving towers are squared.

20. The Cathar heresy had flourished in Lot and Languedoc during the twelfth and early thirteenth centuries. Like the earlier Bogomils the Cathars were duallists, and for decades their church coexisted with the Catholics.

21. Anthony Bek, Prince Bishop of Durham, was a significant figure in the later years of Edward I.

22. The body of the mid-fourteenth-century knight Bartholomew Burghersh demonstrates how constant and sustained training in arms developed the muscles of the right arm considerably, producing an effect akin to deformity and an increase in length. See Prestwich, M., *The Three Edwards* (London, 1980), pp. 137–138.

23. From *The Vows of the Heron*, a late Anglo-Norman poem, written c.1338. See Whiting, B.J., *Speculum*, XX (July 1945), pp. 261–278.

Chapter 2. The Reign of Henry III

1. Burne, op. cit., p. 57.
2. The son of John's brother Geoffrey.
3. She was already promised to Guy de Lusignan and subsequently married, as her second husband, Hugh X of Lusignan.
4. A characteristic which his son Edward I inherited. Though he wrote in the fourteenth century, Trevet's father was a member of the judiciary in the reign of Henry III.
5. It was Edward the Confessor who had founded Westminster Abbey.
6. The image of the 'Two Tablets' probably represented the church victorious and synagogue vanquished; in such representations the synagogue is shown as a woman with broken staff, holding the tablets of law which suggested the Jews' stubbornness and intransigence. The image became so associated with anti-Semitic motifs that it was adopted as the yellow 'Jew badge' which those of the Hebrew persuasion were obliged to wear sewn onto clothing.
7. Carpenter, D., *The Battles of Lewes and Evesham, 1264–1265* (Keele, 1987), p. 8.
8. Maddicott, J.R., *Simon de Montfort* (Cambridge, 1994), p. 174; see the extract from Simon's will.
9. Now Zadar in Croatia.
10. Edward was 6ft 2in (1.88m) tall, a respectable height in any age, and very tall for the thirteenth century.
11. From the inscription on the king's tomb though this appellation may be a sixteenth-century addition; it has not won Edward many admirers in Scotland.
12. Prestwich, M., *Edward I* (London, 1988), p. 3.
13. The marriage was both long and successful, and Eleanor bore the king sixteen children.

14. Peter of Savoy (1203–1268), known as *The Little Charlemagne*, built the Savoy Palace in London, which survived till the Peasants' Revolt, and succeeded his brother Boniface to the archbishopric of Canterbury.
15. Prestwich, op. cit., p. 22.
16. John fitz Geoffrey (1206–1258), Justiciar of Ireland and a leading reformer.
17. See Kingsford, C.L., *The Song of Lewes*, as reviewed by G.W. Prothero in *English Historical Review*, VII, no. 25 (January 1892), pp. 144–146.
18. Simon was reluctant to swear the oath supporting the Provisions of Oxford as he took the important business of oath-taking most seriously. He never deviated from the obligations once sworn and is said to have expressed some scorn in relation to the conduct of his English magnatial contemporaries. He is said to have remarked in the course of a row with de Clare in 1259, 'I do not want to live or have dealings with men so fickle and deceitful.' See Maddicott, op. cit., p. 180.
19. First Lord Seagrave (c.1238–1295).
20. Constable of Winchester Castle (c.1235–c.1269).
21. Louis IX of France (1214–1270) was famed for his deep piety and benevolence, which brought about his canonization. The second of the two crusades he led ended in disaster at Mansourah, where he was outfought and captured by the Egyptians. A noted patron of the arts and respected arbiter, he was scarcely likely, as a sovereign, to countenance such comprehensive fetters being placed on the king's right to rule.

Chapter 3. Lewes (1) – The Campaign

1. De Montfort had taken the precaution of extracting oaths of loyalty from the burgesses: see *Chronicle of Dunstable Priory* in Luard, *Annales Monastici*, III, p. 226.
2. *Chronicle of Dunstable Priory*, p. 230; Rothwell, H., ed., *Chronicle of Walter of Guisborough* [also referred to as Walter of Hemmingburgh], Camden Society, LXXXIX (1967), p. 191;

Fitz Thedmar, A., [London alderman], *Chronicles of the Mayors and Sheriffs of London*, trans. H.T. Riley (London, 1863), p. 62.

3. The king's favourite Hugh Despenser clearly relished oppressing Roger Mortimer, Earl of March, with dire consequences. See Mortimer, I., *The Greatest Traitor: The Life of Sir Roger Mortimer, Ruler of England, 1327–1330* (London, 2004).

4. Carpenter, op. cit., p. 14.

5. *Chronicle of Dunstable Priory*, p. 231.

6. The prisoners were in fact mutilated. See Oman, op. cit., p. 422.

7. The Cinque Ports were a confederation of coastal trading towns in Kent and Sussex, originally Hastings, New Romney, Hythe, Dover and Sandwich, supported by the twin towns of Winchelsea and Rye, plus as later additions seven other ports, appendages of the others: Lydd, Folkestone, Faversham, Margate, Deal, Ramsgate and Tenterden. For the *Chronicle of Battle Abbey*, see Bemont, *Simon de Montfort* (1884).

8. *Chronicle of Battle Abbey*, pp. 375–376; see the continuation of the work of Matthew Paris by a monk of St Albans, in Luard, H.R., ed., *Flores Historiarum*, II, Rolls Series (1890), pp. 489–490; Wykes (linked to Richard of Cornwall and retired to Osney Abbey), *Chronicle*, in Luard, *Annales Monastici*, IV, pp. 147–148.

9. *Chronicle of Battle Abbey*, p. 376.

10. Rothwell, op. cit., p. 192; Winchester (connected to Winchester Cathedral Priory) in *Annales Monastici*, I, p. 451.

11. Oman, op. cit., p. 424.

12. Carpenter, op. cit., p. 18.

13. Ibid., p. 19. Carpenter draws heavily on the Gilson fragment, so named after the chronicle source discovered and published by J.P. Gilson ('An Unpublished Notice of the Battle of Lewes', *English Historical Review*, XI, 1896); this offers an alternative and compelling account of certain aspects of the preliminaries and battle.

14. Stephen Bersted of Chichester: elevated in 1262, not noted prior to this as a Montfortian partisan, but one who was clearly influenced by the arguments in favour of the baronial cause. See Maddicott, op. cit., pp. 267–268.
15. Burne, Colonel A., *More Battlefields of England* (London, 1952), p. 102.
16. Denholm-Young, N., *Richard of Cornwall* (Oxford, 1987), p. 129.
17. Now the small woodlands of Longwood, Warningore Wood and the Wilderness. See Carpenter, op. cit., p. 20.
18. Ibid., p. 21.
19. Carpenter with the aid of local historians discovered the location of Boxholte on a map of 1772.
20. Halliwell, J.O., ed., *Chronicle of William de Rishanger of the Barons' Wars*, Camden Society (1840), p. 31.
21. The chronicler claims that Simon did not waste the 13th but used the time to drill his men and fix them in their divisions. See ibid., p. 31.
22. The racecourse is a mid-eighteenth-century addition.

Chapter 4. Lewes (2) – The Battle

1. Burne, *More Battlefields*, p. 104.
2. Carpenter, op. cit., p. 30.
3. Ibid., p. 30.
4. Ibid., p. 30.
5. Ibid., pp. 22–23.
6. Burne, op. cit., pp. 105–106.
7. Carpenter, op. cit., p. 28.
8. Ibid., p. 28.
9. It was Blaauw who identified the mill *suelligi* with *sullingus* – a measure of land equal in proportions to a hide; thus the mill become the 'mill of the Hide' and is placed in the area known as the Hides. Carpenter argues compellingly that the correct labelling is as the mill of Snelling, a very common personal name in and around Lewes in the thirteenth century. See Carpenter, op. cit., pp. 29–30.

10. Gilson, op. cit., p. 522; Guisborough (Rothwell, op. cit.), it should be noted, places de Bohun with the king's brigade on the left, and we know he was wounded and taken, which suggests this may be right.
11. Rothwell, op. cit., p. 194.
12. Burne, op. cit., p. 106.
13. The Battle of Neville's Cross fought by Durham in 1346 between English and Scots is a case in point.
14. Winchester, op. cit., p. 452.
15. Burne, op. cit., p. 107.
16. Stubbs, E., ed., *The Historical Works of Gervase of Canterbury*, II, Rolls Series (1880), p. 237.
17. In the event he did not honour this commitment and this failure proved very much an 'own goal'.

Chapter 5. Evesham (1) – The Campaign

1. Kingsford, C.L., ed., *The Song of Lewes* (Oxford, 1890), I. 370.
2. Ibid., II. 479–526 et seq.
3. Maddicott, op. cit., p. 284.
4. Ibid., p. 291.
5. Ibid., p. 310.
6. Wykes, op. cit., pp. 153–154.
7. The marriage did not take place until many years later, 1278. Simon the Younger had been in hot pursuit of a most eligible widow, Isabella de Fors, Countess of Devon, widow to the late Earl of Albemarle. The lady was clearly not excited by the prospect, being prepared to flee into Wales in order to give her suitor the slip.
8. The tourney at this time was a far rougher affair than its more decorous successor; injuries and even death were by no means uncommon.
9. Oman, op. cit., p. 434.
10. Blaauw, W.H., *The Barons' War, including the Battles of Lewes and Evesham*, 2nd edn (London, 1871), p. 271, n. 4.
11. Cox, D.C., *The Battle of Evesham: A New Account*, Vale of Evesham History Society (1988), p. 7.

12. *Chronica de Mailros* [Melrose], Bannatyne Club (Edinburgh, 1835), pp. 198–199; Halliwell, op. cit., p. 541.
13. Carpenter, op. cit., p. 50.
14. Oman, op. cit., p. 436.
15. Wright, W.A., ed., *The Metrical Chronicle of Robert of Gloucester*, II, Rolls Series (1887), ll. 11688–11689.
16. Cox, op. cit., p. 8.
17. Rothwell, op. cit., p. 199.
18. Cox, op. cit., p. 8.
19. Ibid., p. 9.

Chapter 6. Evesham (2) – The Battle

1. Cox, op. cit., p. 10.
2. Evesham Chronicle (which contains important local traditions of the battle and its location), Oxford, Bodleian Library, MS Laud Misc., 529, ff. 70–71, f. 70.
3. Ibid., f. 71.
4. Carpenter, op. cit., p. 54.
5. Ibid., p. 54.
6. Ibid., p. 55.
7. This is shown on a surviving map from 1675. See Carpenter, op. cit., p. 57.
8. A road or track is clearly shown on the same map of 1675.
9. Guisborough (Rothwell, op. cit.) records that when the royalist forces were first sighted from the abbey tower, they were seen approaching from three sides; this suggests the prince's corps had not yet recrossed the Avon. As Tony Spicer observes, Green Hill may not be the hill Wykes refers to – there is another candidate about a mile north and slightly west, smaller in size but adequate for the purposes of concealment. Travelling from Mosham Meadow toward Green Hill it is about half a mile on the left, on a minor road towards Lenchwick.
10. The bishop quit Evesham for his manor of Blockley. He appears badly shaken by the disaster, though he later ostensibly repented of his support for the baronial faction and received absolution from the papal legate; he died the

following February. See Cox, op. cit., p. 13.

11. The gradient is no more than 1 in 23. See Cox, op. cit., p. 14.
12. Halliwell, op. cit., p. 543.
13. De Clare had famously red hair. See Cox, op. cit. p. 14, and Carpenter, op. cit., p. 59.
14. Wykes, op. cit., p. 173.
15. Rothwell, op. cit., p. 201; Melrose, op. cit., pp. 200–201.
16. Carpenter, op. cit., p. 64.
17. Cox places the site of the earl's last stand at 'God's Croft', which is identified with the nineteenth-century property the Croft, which stands nearly 1,000 yards south of Battle Well. I have to reject this as being too far south. Cox believes the royalists attacked first and the baronial army was pushed some way down the hill; I consider this unlikely. See Cox, op. cit., pp. 16–17.
18. Carpenter, op. cit., p. 64.
19. Cox, op. cit., p. 17.
20. Included in the thieves' ungodly haul was a very fine psalter, commissioned by the abbey some fifteen years earlier, and said to be one of the finest of English illuminations. It is next heard of in the ownership of Richard of Cornwall. See Cox, op. cit., p. 17.
21. The blood-decked precincts remained tainted till an appropriate cleansing was performed by Anian, Bishop of Bangor, in 1295.
22. Cox, op. cit., p. 18.
23. Ibid., p. 18.
24. Within the abbey the choir lay beneath the crossing, with the presbytery and high altar to the east; the latter had a raised floor, being constructed over a crypt below. A saint's tomb already lay within or under the choir. The Evesham dead were interred just west of the steps leading to the presbytery; this location has, of course vanished, but Cox places the site of the tombs some 15 yards south-east of the point where a modern fence links to a wall joining chapter-house arch to bell tower. See Cox., op. cit., pp. 18–19.

Chapter 7. Legacy
1. Prestwich, *Edward I*, p. 52.
2. These included Warin de Bassingbourne, Hamo Lestrange, Leyburn, John de Vaux and the Savoyard Otto de Grandson. See Prestwich, op. cit., p. 54.
3. Chronicle of Waverley Abbey, in Luard, *Annales Monastici*, II, p. 366.
4. Wykes, op. cit., pp. 189–190.
5. Prestwich, op. cit., p. 57.
6. Wykes, op. cit., pp. 195–196.
7. The de Vescis were, at this time, lords of Alnwick; the Percys, who were to become the dominant magnatial family in the north during the fourteenth century, had not yet acquired an interest.
8. Ibid., pp. 197–198.
9. Maddicott, op. cit., pp. 370–371.

Appendices
1. De Laborderie, O., 'The Last Hours of Simon de Montfort: A New Account', *English Historical Review*, CXV (April 2000), p. 378.
2. None of the chroniclers name Mortimer as being present at Kenilworth; both Tony Spicer and I are here relying on Inherent Military Probability, a course fraught with risk for the historian! In the absence of clear evidence to the contrary, however, the assumptions concerning Mortimer's movements merit serious consideration.
3. Chronicle of Westminster Abbey, written in the 14th century but containing earlier records, in Luard, *Flores Historiarum*.

Select Bibliography

Primary sources

Bemont, C., *Simon de Montfort* (Paris, 1884)

Blaauw, W.H., 'On the Early History of Lewes Priory . . . with Extracts from a MS Chronicle', *Sussex Archaeological Collections*, II (1849)

Calendar of Liberate Rolls 1260–1267 (HMSO, 1961)

Calendar of Patent Rolls, 1258–1266 (HMSO, 1910)

Chronica de Mailros, Bannatyne Club (Edinburgh, 1835)

Chronicles of Lanercost, trans. H. Maxwell (Glasgow, 1913)

Close Rolls, 1261–1264 (HMSO, 1936)

Close Rolls, 1264–1268 (HMSO, 1937)

Ellis, H., ed., *Chronica Johannis de Oxenedes*, Rolls Series (1890)

Fitz Thedmar, A., *Chronicles of the Mayors and Sheriffs of London*, trans. H.T. Riley (London, 1863)

Gilson, J.P., 'An Unpublished Notice of the Battle of Lewes' [the Gilson Fragment], *English Historical Review*, XI (1896)

Halliwell, J.O., ed., *Chronicle of William de Rishanger of the Barons' Wars*, Camden Society (1840)

Hog, T., ed., *Nicholai Triveti Annales* (London, 1845)

Howlett, R., ed., *Chronicles of the Reigns of Stephen, Henry II and Richard I*, II, Rolls Series (1885)

Kingsford, C.L., ed., *The Song of Lewes* (Oxford, 1890)

Luard, H.R., ed., *Annales Monastici*, 5 vols, Rolls Series (1865–1869)

——, ed., *Flores Historiarum*, II, Rolls Series (1890)

Paris, Matthew (Matthaei Parisiensis), *Monachi Sancti Albani: Chronica Majorca*, ed. H.R. Luard, Rolls Series (1872–1883)

Rothwell, H., ed., *Chronicle of Walter of Guisborough*, Camden Society, LXXXIX (1967)

Stapleton, T., ed., *Chronica maiorum et vicecomitum Londarium*, Camden Society (1846)

Stubbs, E., ed., *The Historical Works of Gervase of Canterbury*, II, Rolls Series (1880)

——, ed., *Chronicles of the Reigns of Edward I and Edward II*, I, Rolls Series (1882)

Trinity College, Cambridge, R5/40, ff. 75–75*v* [a fragment brought to light by Dr. D.W. Burton, possibly connected with Gilbert de Clare]

Wright, W.A., ed., *Metrical Chronicle of Robert of Gloucester*, II, Rolls Series (1887)

Secondary Sources

Barbour, R., *The Knight and Chivalry* (London, 1974)

Barr, J., 'The Battle of Evesham, 1265', *Miniature Wargames* (March 1991)

Bartlett, C., *The English Longbowman, 1313–1515* (Oxford, 1995)

Beamish, Sir T. (Lord Chelwood), *Battle Royal* (London, 1965)

Bemont, C., *Simon de Montfort* (Oxford, 1930)

Blaauw, W.H., *The Barons' War, including the Battles of Lewes and Evesham*, 2nd edn (1871)

Blair, C., *European Armour* (London, 1958)

Bradbury, J., *The Medieval Archer* (New York, 1985)

Brent, C., *Historic Lewes and Its Buildings* (Lewes, 1987)

Burne, Colonel A., *The Battlefields of England* (London, 1951)

——, *More Battlefields of England* (London, 1952)

Carpenter, D., 'What Happened in 1258?', in *War and Government in the Middle Ages: Essays in Honour of J.O. Prestwich*, eds. J. Gillingham and J.C. Holt (Woodbridge, 1984)

——, 'Simon de Montfort and the Mise of Lewes', *Bulletin of the Institute of Historical Research*, LVIII (1985)

——, *The Battles of Lewes and Evesham 1264–1265* (Keele, 1987)

Contamine, P., *War in the Middle Ages*, trans. M. Jones (Oxford, 1984)

Cox, D.C., *The Battle of Evesham: A New Account* (Vale of Evesham Historical Society, 1988)

Davis, R.H.C., *The Medieval Warhorse* (London, 1989)

De Laborderie, O., 'The Last Hours of Simon de Montfort: A
  New Account', *English Historical Review*, CXV (April 2000)
Denholm-Young, N., *Richard of Cornwall* (Oxford, 1947)
Devries, K., *Infantry Warfare in the Early Fourteenth Century:
  Discipline, Tactics and Technology* (Woodbridge, 1996)
Dimmock, H.L.F., 'Some Musings of the Battle of Lewes AD
  1264', *Journal of the Royal Artillery*, LXI, no. 2 (July 1934)
Ducklin, K., and J. Waller, *Sword Fighting* (London, 2001)
English Heritage, *Battlefield Report: Evesham, 1265* (1995)
——, *Battlefield Report: Lewes, 1264* (1995)
Evans, J. (ed.), *The Flowering of the Middle Ages* (London, 1998)
Gravett, C., *Medieval Siege Warfare* (London, 1990)
Halliwell, J.O., *The Miracles of Simon de Montfort*, Camden
  Society (1840)
Hyland, A., *The Medieval Warhorse from Byzantium to the
  Crusades* (Gloucs., 1994)
Keegan, J., *The Face of Battle* (London, 1976)
Keen, M., *Medieval Warfare: A History* (Oxford, 1990)
Kingsford, C.L., *The Song of Lewes* (Oxford, 1890)
Lemmon, C.H., 'The Field of Lewes', *The Battle of Lewes, 1264:
  Its Place in English History* (Lewes, 1964)
Maddicott, J.R., 'The Mise of Lewes, 1264', *English Historical
  Review*, XCVIII (1983)
Mann, E.L., *The Battle of Lewes* (Lewes, 1976)
Mersey, D., 'The Battle of Evesham, 1265', *Miniature Wargames*
  (November 2000)
Morris, J.E., *The Welsh Wars of Edward I* (Oxford, 1901)
——, *Mounted Infantry in Medieval Warfare*, Royal Historical
  Society, 3rd series, VIII (1914)
Nicolle, D., *A Medieval Warfare Source Book* (London, 1999)
Norman, A.V.B., and D. Pottinger, *English Weapons & Warfare,
  449–1660* (London, 1966)
Oakeshott, R.E., *A Knight and His Armour* (London, 1961)
——, *A Knight and His Horse* (London, 1962)
——, *A Knight and His Weapons* (London, 1964)
——, *A Knight and His Castle* (London, 1965)

Oman, Sir C., *The Art of War in the Middle Ages*, vol. 1 (London, 1924)

Prestwich, M., *Edward I* (London, 1988)

——, *Armies and Warfare in the Middle Ages* (London, 1996)

Prothero, G.W., *The Life of Simon de Montfort, Earl of Leicester: With Special Reference to the Parliamentary History of His Time* (London, 1877)

Ramsay, Sir J.H., *The Dawn of the Constitution* (Oxford, 1908)

Rudge, E.J., *Short Account of the History and Antiquities of Evesham* (1820)

Smith, R., *The Utility of Force: The Art of War in the Modern World* (London, 2005)

Smurthwaite, D., *Battlefields of Britain* (London 1984)

Tindal, W., *The History and Antiquities of the Abbey and Borough of Evesham, compiled chiefly from MS. in the British Museum* (Evesham, 1794)

Treharne, R.F., *Simon de Montfort and Baronial Reform* (London, 1986)

Wagner, P., and S. Hand, *Medieval Sword and Shield* (California, 2003)

Williams, D., 'Simon de Montfort and His Adherents', in *England in the Thirteenth Century*, ed. W.M. Ormrod (Woodbridge, 1985)

Wise, T., *Medieval Heraldry* (Oxford, 1983)

Index